PRAISE FOR THRIVE

"We live in a time when uncertainty is the order of the day. *THRIVE* is a must-read for all who strive to grow intellectually and to succeed through the opportunities an uncertain world offers."

—Ken Langone
Founder, Home Depot
American Billionaire and Philanthropist

"Talk about the right book for the right time! What I liked most about *THRIVE* are the case studies of real companies and real people who weathered the storms and emerged more successful than before. *THRIVE* is both practical and inspirational. I've ordered copies for my entire team."

—Bill Cates, CSP, CPAE
Founder, The Cates Academy for Relationship Marketing
Author of *Radical Relevance*

"In *THRIVE*, Meridith weaves in 250 years of business history to show how resilient businesses and people find opportunities in every situation. This is a must-read to gain ideas and perspective in a sea of change."

—Mary C. Kelly, PhD
CEO, Productive Leaders
Author of *The Five Minute Leadership Guide*

"You do not merely read this book; you read, you think, you develop next steps. Meridith does a masterful job of detailing companies doing it right and then goes further by adding her insights to create a playbook of what you need to do. Perfect book for the time we're in right now!"

—Mark Hunter, CSP
"The Sales Hunter"
Author of *A Mind For Sales*

"The only certainty in business is there will be times of great uncertainty. It's how you react when your world—or the world—doesn't go as planned that determines your future. Meridith studies how companies have thrived in their uncertain times to become global market leaders and shares the proven success strategies that you can implement in your business to do the same. If there was ever a time where our world needed this book, it's now. Read it. Study it. And thrive!"

—Sam Richter, CSP, CPAE
Hall of Fame Speaker, Bestselling Author,
and Technology Entrepreneur

"*THRIVE* is a must-read for anyone looking to grow their business, the ultimate blueprint for how to pivot during times of ambiguity. Meridith Elliott Powell is one of THE top keynote speakers in the world, and the way she weaves in her unique combination of storytelling, wisdom, research, insights, and wonderful sense of humor is so compelling. Every solopreneur, small business owner, manager, and C-suite executive needs to read this book. I can't recommend it enough!"

—Ross Bernstein, CSP
Inspirational Business Speaker and
Bestselling Sports Author

"With *THRIVE*, author Meridith Elliott Powell offers us a prescient and timely book. She searches business history to show us precisely how her case study companies thrived in times of uncertainty, but also gives us a practical and proven blueprint for moving into the future with thoughtful strategies and bold action. A wealth of information and insight, *THRIVE* is required reading for anyone who wants to play a bigger game in work and life!""

—Libby Gill
Executive Coach
Award-Winning Author of *You Unstuck* and
The Hope-Driven Leader

"The minute I met banker Meridith Elliott Powell more than 25 years ago, I felt she was destined for greatness. With several bestsellers under her belt and a speaking presence like no other, I have been proven correct. In her latest classic, *THRIVE: Strategies to Turn Uncertainty into Competitive Advantage*, Meredith shows us how to take on the challenges of doubt, ambiguity and insecurity and offers nine practical strategies to turn uncertainty into a personal and business competitive advantage. Right time, right place, right book. This one is a must-read.

—Jack Hubbard
Chief Experience Officer, St. Meyer & Hubbard

"Perhaps there is nothing that breeds insecurity more deeply than a sense of uncertainty. This book lays out a step-by-step strategy and plan to be able to leverage uncertainty to your advantage. In a time when people are searching for a clear path to competitive advantage and personal and business success, Meridith Elliott Powell shows us a clear, compelling way forward. Read it, apply it, live it. You will be glad you did."

—Mike Staver
CEO, The Staver Group

THRIVE

Strategies to Turn Uncertainty into
COMPETITIVE
ADVANTAGE

MERIDITH ELLIOTT POWELL

Published and distributed by:
SOUND WISDOM
P.O. Box 310
Shippensburg, PA 17257-0310
717-530-2122

info@soundwisdom.com

www.soundwisdom.com

While efforts have been made to verify information contained in this publication, neither the author nor the publisher assumes any responsibility for errors, inaccuracies, or omissions. While this publication is chock-full of useful, practical information; it is not intended to be legal or accounting advice. All readers are advised to seek competent lawyers and accountants to follow laws and regulations that may apply to specific situations. The reader of this publication assumes responsibility for the use of the information. The author and publisher assume no responsibility or liability whatsoever on the behalf of the reader of this publication.

Library of Congress Control Number: 2021931046

ISBN 13 HC: 978-1-64095-282-9

ISBN 13 TP: 978-1-64095-309-3

ISBN 13 eBook: 978-1-64095-283-6

For Worldwide Distribution, Printed in the U.S.A.

1 2 3 4 5 6 7 8 / 25 24 23 22 21

DEDICATION

This book is dedicated to the companies and leaders who served as the inspiration for this idea, this formula and my newfound passion for helping others turn uncertainty into competitive advantage.

It is also dedicated to those who provided valuable support throughout the entire development process:

- To my sister, Beth, who listens to me endlessly share my ideas and then somehow shapes them into powerful strategies.
- To my editor, Susan, for her ability to be as excited about my ideas as I am and for her commitment to help me bring them to fruition.

- To my best friend, Sue, who selflessly supports me, believes in me, and opens doors and opportunities for me that I could never access myself.
- And to my husband, Rob, for his patience when I get engrossed in projects, his belief in me, and for always, always being my biggest cheerleader.

CONTENTS

FOREWORD

BY TOM FAZIO

I have known Meridith for more than three decades, and I've always been impressed with her knowledge and dedication to the principles of hard work and commitment. She is an avid supporter of our local Boys & Girls Club, serving as the president, an ongoing consultant and a keynote speaker at the regional conference. Her generosity of time and sense of caring have touched many lives.

After reviewing this book, I am very impressed with her thought process and the development of a formula that is so clear and easily implemented. She totally understands how an organization can meet the challenges of what seems to be the "new normal"—thriving in uncertainty.

I know firsthand how uncertainty can impact a business. I entered the golf course construction and design industry in the mid-1960s and started my own company,

Fazio Design, in 1972. From the very beginning, we had to learn the lesson of flexibility.

Our corporate offices were originally in Philadelphia. When we realized the majority of golf courses were being built in the southwest and southeast, we moved our offices to Florida and Arizona to accommodate our clients. Without that switch, we would probably have lost a significant amount of business.

When the energy crisis occurred in the mid-1970s, very few new golf courses were being built. We shifted our business model to target renovations of existing courses. That was followed by the global economic transformation of the 1980s, which pushed us to redefine our scope and develop new ways to attract projects from around the world.

In the late 1990s and early 2000s, we faced the fallout from the dot-com bubble burst, a stock market crisis and the tragedy of 9/11. Investor confidence tanked, and many second-home golf communities felt the crush. We responded by consolidating our offices into a single location in North Carolina, and our designers collaborated to work on a single project at a time.

The success of golf communities continued to fluctuate with the 2007 subprime mortgage crisis and the subsequent Great Recession of 2008. As you might imagine, the pandemic of 2020 threw another wrench into our plans.

Through all of those episodes of uncertainty, our business had to be flexible while our products remained the same. Quality and consistency remained as our core values. Whether the stock market was up or down, our clients chose us because of our reputation. They trusted us to do the right things for the right reasons despite the state of the global economy.

We survived, but it wasn't always easy. If I had known about Meridith's formula for thriving in uncertainty early in my career, I could have eliminated many, many days of anguish, worry and frustration.

The amazing insights and real-world solutions found in this book can provide enormous value to professionals who are struggling to manage a constant flow of uncertainty inside and outside of their companies. If they apply Meridith's formula and incorporate her wisdom, they will enjoy immediate results and the lasting benefit of long-term success.

Tom Fazio

Tom Fazio, ASGCA, is a world-renowned golf course architect and founder of Fazio Design (www.FazioDesign.com). He has developed over 120 golf courses, with more of them ranked in the Top 100 in the US than anyone else in the business. He was named "Best Modern Day Golf Course Architect" by *Golf Digest* magazine three times and received top honors from the Golf Course Superintendents Association of America with the Old Tom Morris Award.

Uncertainty and the State of
AMERICAN BUSINESS

This book was written as a guide, a reference for what you need to know to completely shift how you think and feel about uncertainty. **THRIVE** will take you on a journey to better understand uncertainty, its impact on your business and the customer experience, and the massive potential that exists in an uncertain marketplace.

Throughout the pages of this book, you will encounter powerful stories about companies and leaders who have not only pushed through challenging times, but thrived through them, which will inspire you to take action. You will also gain peace of mind, knowing that uncertainty and challenge are not cataclysmic events; they are just part of being in business. Every generation experiences them.

THRIVE is based on two levels of research:

- *Qualitative – historical and narrative.* We invested significant time into identifying, studying, and talking with the companies highlighted in this book so that we could gather their stories, learn about their challenges, and detail what was uncovered.

- *Quantitative – survey and data-based.* In 2020, we hired The Center For Generational Kinetics to undertake a thorough survey- and data-driven research project to help us understand, verify and prove the impact of uncertainty on leaders, organizations and American business today. The Center For Generational Kinetics is one of the most prominent research firms in the country, working with today's leading companies in every major industry. Their research has been featured in *The Wall Street Journal*, *The New York Times*, *Fortune Magazine* and many others. Our goal with the research was to test both the findings and strategies we uncovered from working with and interviewing the featured companies and developing our 9-Step Formula. While we knew from the qualitative research and our own experience that these were the strategies that would transform any leader or company challenged with uncertainty, we wanted to go a level deeper and further prove the results.

The goals of our study were as follows:

- To understand the influence of uncertainty in business and test how business leaders think about and navigate uncertainty.
- To further explore the differences between businesses and business leaders that are proactively conditioned for change and uncertainty and those that are reactive to it.
- To test the importance of flexibility, adaptability, and objectivity when dealing with uncertainty in business.
- To verify if the strategies in our 9-Step Formula were the steps that businesses and leaders need to take to redefine how they think, act and find success in the face of uncertainty.

More than 800 business leaders, CEOs and C-suite professionals took part in this study, with an equal participation of male and female leaders. Over 200 of the leaders were from companies with more than 1,000 employees. The age range of participants was from 30 to 65—managers, directors, CEOs and C-suite professionals from every generation were represented.

The results of the study were profound. They further proved the need for this book and the value of the 9-Step Formula. They also demonstrated the importance of businesses and leaders learning to shift their beliefs and actions related to uncertainty.

Here are some high-level findings from the research:

- 76% of business leaders say that uncertainty is one of the most important yet least understood concepts in business.
- 84% of business leaders say that being able to lead through uncertainty effectively is more important than ever before.
- 84% of business leaders say that handling uncertainty well is a sign of professionalism.
- Creating engaged teams, building succession plans and understanding how to balance being highly focused and highly flexible are the most helpful skills leaders need to successfully navigate uncertainty.
- 84% of business leaders say that leaders who proactively look at, manage and communicate change are more likely to be successful.
- 80% of business leaders say that you can adapt to change without compromising your company's values.
- 78% of leaders say that being flexible impacts your company's ability to be successful in uncertain times.
- The most important qualities of a team that looks at change proactively vary dramatically by generation. For older Millennials, it's a team of strong communicators and good listeners.

For Gen X, it's a team that's engaging, and for Boomers, it's a team that views change as an opportunity, embraces reality, and asks for and accepts feedback.

- 84% of business leaders say that having established core values is essential to the long-term success of a business.

- Making a clear connection between a company's core values and its actions is the best way for business leaders to communicate those core values to their employees. This belief is consistent across generations and genders.

- 70% of business leaders say that a good company culture will make employees stay longer at a job they don't like.

- 83% of business leaders say that it's important to step away from their company and look at things objectively in order to make more productive decisions.

- 57% of business leaders say that other leaders are incapable of looking at their company objectively when making decisions.

- 58% of business leaders rank relevancy in the top three most important qualities of a successful business.

- 88% of business leaders say that relevancy is important or absolutely critical to the long-term success of a business.

So what are the bottom-line findings from this research? And what will you learn from reading this book and implementing our 9-Step Formula?

- Business leaders report feeling that uncertainty threatens the success of their company and impacts their company's performance. In the pages of **THRIVE**, we'll dive into the impact uncertainty has on business, the customer experience and overall performance. You'll understand uncertainty at a deeper level and learn how to make it work for, rather than against, you.

- Three out of four business leaders say that their team would be more valuable if they were better at handling uncertainty. **THRIVE** provides the research and the strategies for how to lead through uncertainty, help your team engage in the process, and build their resilience and agility when it comes to shifts in the marketplace.

- Overwhelmingly, business leaders say that it's important to condition themselves to handle change, and they see clear value in conditioning their employees to handle change. **THRIVE** provides the tools and resources to prime your leaders, your team members and your organization to handle change in the most effective way possible.

- Business leaders believe that a company's culture and core values are critical to their ability to handle *uncertainty*. **THRIVE** details how to actively use your core values to further develop your team, enhance your culture and increase performance.

- Interestingly, business leaders understand the importance of looking at their company objectively in order to make more productive decisions, but they also find this difficult to do. **THRIVE** equips you with the techniques that will enable you to look at your company objectively, understand what you need to continue to do, recognize what needs to change, and quickly identify what needs to be added.

- Business leaders overwhelmingly say that *relevancy* is important or absolutely critical to the long-term success of a business. **THRIVE** outlines the impact that relevancy can have on business growth and resilience and provides the tools needed to ensure your strategy, your products, your messaging and your team remain relevant.

While uncertainty will remain one of the biggest challenges that leaders and organizations face today, our mission with this book—our passion—has been to help you view uncertainty differently—to see uncertainty as something that does not prevent growth, but actually something that can propel it.

As you read **THRIVE**, you will see the questions you have about uncertainty addressed on every page, you will learn from the companies and leaders that have gone before you, you will gain the solutions you need to push through your biggest obstacles, and you will acquire the strategies and tools you need to consistently turn uncertainty into your competitive advantage.

Enjoy,

Meridith Elliott Powell

INTRODUCTION

A new year, a new decade. So much promise.

Like many of you, I started 2020 strong. By the end of February, I was on track to have my best quarter—and what I believed would be my best year on record since I started my business. The excitement was palpable.

Then, in one week, everything changed.

Those pivotal moments are unforgettable. The declaration of a global pandemic. The stay-at-home orders. The travel lockdown. The promise of my spectacular year circling the drain.

I make my living as a keynote speaker. By definition, I am paid to get on airplanes and travel around the world and engage with thousands of people. That business model instantly became obsolete during the second week of March.

One by one, my speaking engagements were canceled. Potential revenue disappeared. And my once-packed calendar was empty. To add insult to injury, my business model became unworkable. Thanks to COVID-19, worldwide travel and close contact with huge groups of people were no longer an option.

My first response to a business environment decimated by a global pandemic was...well, panic. OK, technically speaking, I might have freaked out a little bit. I had no idea how I was going to generate income. Would I have to sell everything I own on eBay? Could I get a job delivering pizzas?

Then I got mad. I mean *really angry*. This novel coronavirus was not only threatening hundreds of thousands of lives around the world, but it was also personally attacking my business, my goals, and my revenue. Even if I wasn't *infected*, I was deeply *affected*. I felt uncharacteristically powerless. I felt like a victim—but not for long.

I quickly recognized that this situation was completely out of my control. The only thing I *could* control was my response. I knew I needed a strategy.

Did I have one? Nope. This was all-new territory.

Oddly enough, I had spent the last 18 months doing preliminary research for a book about how companies navigate challenges in the business environment. The original concept was to help leaders guide their organizations through economic hardships such as recessions, workforce shortages, or an influx of new competition. I can definitively say that the word "pandemic" never entered the conversation.

But here we were.

I had already completed in-depth interviews with leaders from some of the oldest, most stable companies around the country to find out their secrets to success. Given the context of the current situation, I sensed that the leaders' responses were just as much about how to survive as they were about how to succeed. After all, these corporate giants had made it through wars, stock market crashes, recessions, depressions, cultural upheaval, 9/11, the subprime mortgage crisis. And, yes, the Spanish flu pandemic of 1918.

Perhaps the blueprint for *my* business survival in 2020 was hidden somewhere in all those pages of interview notes.

With my speaking events canceled and the... *ahem*..."luxury" of time, I started pouring through my book research files to look for answers—or at least some inspiration. What specific strategies did these evergreen companies use to stay in business despite centuries of major challenges? How did they thrive when so many others went under? And most importantly, were there any common threads?

I had to analyze these business models on a much deeper level than I initially intended. However, the similarities I found were mind-blowing.

DISCOVERING THE FORMULA

When I finished my in-depth review of these companies, I compiled my insights, cross-referenced the results, and worked to distill their proven wisdom. What did I end up with?

I found a list of nine concise strategies that seemed to create an unwritten formula for thriving in the midst of uncertainty. This was not at all what I expected when I started the project in 2018, but it was somehow even more compelling.

To be quite frank, I wasn't completely sure this formula would apply to me as a solo entrepreneur. But I was desperate—and willing to take the bet. It was time to drink my own Kool-Aid, so to speak.

Fast-forward four months.

After social distancing guidelines choked the life out of my balance sheet, this unique collection of strategies helped me turn my business around in a dramatic way. They also changed my approach to this book. Instead of just sharing a formula used by some highly respected, powerhouse companies, I now had firsthand experience with the application and its success. My level of passion about this writing project increased exponentially.

The formula was simple, although not necessarily easy to implement. It required discipline, consistency and courage. But, most importantly, it worked. I saw it happen.

I don't know what kind of uncertainty and adversity are looming over your professional life (or the life of your company) as you read this book right now, but I know one thing for sure. The insights in the pages ahead can give you the preparation and direction you need to handle it. No matter what it is.

Minor crisis or major catastrophe, the same formula applies.

Are you a current or future leader? An entrepreneur, executive team member or sole proprietor? Do you work for a small family business or a Fortune 500 company? Again, the same formula works.

If you are diligent about applying these strategies during good times and bad, you can capture a unique competitive advantage. Even better, you'll gain a secret weapon to help you outlast whatever uncertainty comes next.

PRESENTING THE INFORMATION

So what can you expect to find as you make your way through this book?

In **Chapter One**, I explore the broader concept of uncertainty—the challenges, the perceptions and the impact. I also include an uncertainty timeline that will give you an interesting historical perspective on this subject and, hopefully, a little peace of mind. There's something calming about the realization that uncertainty is *normal, cyclical and expected.* For hundreds of years, businesses have been enduring situations much tougher than what we are going through today. Survival *and* success are possible.

In **Chapters Two through Ten**, I provide detailed descriptions of the nine strategies that create the formula for thriving in uncertainty. Each chapter starts with a real-world case study—a story about the journey of a trailblazing company and its smart, resilient leaders. I explain how these organizations were founded, the challenges they faced, and the approaches they used to survive.

After each story, I highlight the key parts of the strategy they used and give you guidelines on how you can apply that approach to your own situation as a current or future business leader.

Chapter Eleven offers you a step-by-step action plan for combining these strategies to implement the formula for thriving in uncertainty. You'll have access to valuable tools and worksheets that can streamline your efforts and give your organization a distinct competitive advantage. *(Available for free at www.ValueSpeaker.com.)*

Finally, **Chapter Twelve** provides you with a roadmap for translating the book's business strategies into a formula for managing uncertainty on a personal level. The parallels may surprise you, but the outcomes are equally impressive.

BEGINNING THE JOURNEY

Ready to dive in?

When you finish this book, you will think about uncertainty in a totally different way. You'll no longer see it as something that prevents growth, but as something that actually propels it. You'll understand how to stop allowing uncertainty to hold you back. Instead, you'll learn how to turn it into something you can control and even leverage.

The leaders responsible for companies that stood the test of time discovered that opportunity is hiding in the midst of uncertainty. If you know how to search for it and take advantage of it, you and your business can also thrive and be poised for epic, lasting success.

CHAPTER ONE

Unpack the Concept of
UNCERTAINTY

I'm fascinated by the concept of *uncertainty* in the business environment. How C-suite executives and leaders think about it, react to it, and deal with it. The psychology behind all of that. The impact of those perceptions on the bottom line.

After extensively studying this concept, I've drawn some interesting conclusions. The main one? If you want to give your organization the best possible chance for long-term success, it's time to get more comfortable with uncertainty.

In this chapter, I want to share with you **four important insights** I've gleaned about the uncomfortable-yet-inevitable state of uncertainty in the business world.

1. UNCERTAINTY IS AN EMOTIONAL SUBJECT.

No big surprise here: Leaders aren't wild about "best guesses." They want as many facts as possible before making decisions, especially when the outcomes could have an impact on their revenue, their budgets, their teams or their own jobs. They fully recognize that variables are involved, and they use detailed spreadsheets to make multiple projections.

Given a choice between the known and the unknown, the vast majority of professionals would select the former. Unfortunately, we don't always have an option. And that can produce increased **frustration**.

To be fair, some level of uncertainty exists for all of us at any moment in time.

We can't predict when the car will break down or when our Amazon order will be unavoidably delayed. Most of

---

CIVIL WAR (1861)

Uncertainty

- 237 battles fought
- 1,000,000+ casualties amassed
- Infrastructure destroyed
- Social and political upheaval remained

Opportunity

- Centralized federal government established
- National paper currency developed
- Modern medicine emerged
- Nation's first ambulance corps created
- First transcontinental railroad built
- Communication changed with the telegraph

us can go with the flow when faced with those annoying inconveniences. But what happens in the business environment after a natural disaster or a financial crisis? Those events fuel an intense level of uncertainty that can stop us in our tracks. Like toss-out-the-spreadsheets-and-start-from-scratch roadblocks. Complete momentum crashers.

Oh yes, that kind of uncertainty tends to cause some serious **stress**.

In fact, there's concrete proof to back that up. A *Forbes* article recently described a scientific study on this topic that was reported in *Nature Communications*, a leading peer-reviewed journal. This study found that uncertainty *(not knowing what is going to happen)* creates more stress than knowing that something bad is definitely going to happen.

According to the scientists, our bodies can become so consumed with the stress of "what if" that our adrenaline

---

WORLD WAR I (1914)

Uncertainty

- 9.7 million soldiers died worldwide
- 10 million civilians died worldwide
- Fear and violence paralyzed the nation
- Workforce shortages crippled businesses
- Diseases flourished

Opportunity

- Military technology accelerated
- Wireless communication invented
- Workforce restructured to include women
- Manufacturing and GDP increased significantly

spikes, our pupils dilate, and our pulse increases. All of those responses occur at rates that are significantly higher than those associated with the actual negative event.

Translate that into the business setting. A sales executive would experience less stress knowing she will lose her biggest account rather than worrying and speculating about whether she *could* lose it—an outcome that potentially might NOT even happen.

So what's behind that?

Maybe it's a byproduct of our overactive imaginations. One example that comes to mind is Dorothy in the *Wizard of Oz*. She and her pals wasted a lot of time and energy worrying about a scary confrontation with the terrifying, almighty wizard—who ended up being an old guy behind a curtain. Reality wasn't nearly as stressful as

SPANISH FLU (1918)

Uncertainty	Opportunity
• 50 million people died from infections	• Vaccine science advanced
• Medical professionals struggled to respond	• Disease surveillance systems strengthened
• Communication about virus treatments/spread was limited	• Government heal thcare programs established
• Enormous worker shortages occurred due to deaths	• Telephone technology evolved
• Economic crisis ensued	• Communications expanded to better support a heal thcare crisis

uncertainty. I think we've all had that experience at some point in our lives: *Knowing* is just easier than *not knowing*.

To make matters worse, there's another emotion that uncertainty tends to breed: **fear**.

I started noticing that trend a few years ago when I was talking with business owners and leaders. As a point of reference, these conversations occurred during booming economic times. I'd ask them how business was going, and the responses frequently went something like this:

"We're having a great year. Business is growing, banks are lending, and customers are buying. But our luck is bound to run out at some point. There's just so much uncertainty about what's ahead."

What struck me the most was how many different leaders in diverse industries expressed the exact same fear. Even if I never mentioned uncertainty, they did. It was top of mind for virtually everyone I encountered.

GREAT DEPRESSION (1929)

Uncertainty

- Stock market crashed
- Inflation surged
- Enormous debt crippled the nation
- Banks failed
- Unemployment skyrocketed

Opportunity

- Economy restructured
- New relief programs developed
- Emergency Banking Act established
- Securities and Exchange Commission created
- Social Security program developed and deployed

Across the board, uncertainty seems to have become the enemy hiding around the next corner and waiting to steal their prosperity. It's almost like a perpetual threat against enjoying a stable, successful time.

The bigger story, of course, is the impact of these uncertainty-related emotions on leaders and employees alike, as well as the organizations they serve. High-performing teams can't possibly produce at an optimal level if people are continuously distracted by stress, frustration and fear.

Attention spans are shorter. Engagement is shredded. Survival takes precedence over innovation.

Without a doubt, the negative emotions spawned by uncertainty can quickly become counterproductive for everyone involved.

WORLD WAR II (1939)

Uncertainty	Opportunity
• 85 million fatalities occurred globally	• United Nations established
• Bombings, genocide and massacres plagued the world	• Universal Declaration of Human Rights enacted
• Starvation and disease ravaged populations	• Civil Rights movement first launched
	• Aircraft and airlift capacities expanded
	• Military intelligence and cryptography advanced

2. UNCERTAINTY IS A CONSTANT.

If I were an economic meteorologist, I would look you in the eyes with complete confidence and tell you this: *Your forecast includes a 100% chance of uncertainty.*

It's a non-negotiable, inescapable fact of business *and* life. The question is *when*, not *if*.

Every single year delivers its fair share of unexpected surprises and disasters. Without fail. History proves that, over and over. Admittedly, some years seem to serve up a super-sized portion of uncertainty. *(Looking at you, 2020!)*

When we watched the ball drop in Times Square on New Year's Eve 2019, no one could have predicted the complete dumpster fire that became 2020: a global pandemic, economic meltdown, skyrocketing unemployment, shrinking GDP, fierce debates about face masks, and nationwide social unrest. Then, just for fun, we also

---

ENERGY CRISIS (1973)

Uncertainty

- Oil embargo created fuel shortages and high prices
- Gasoline rationing panicked the nation
- Stagnant economy hindered growth
- Inflation raged
- Full-blown recession arrived

Opportunity

- Conservation programs developed
- National speed limit established
- Environmentalism increased
- Domestic oil production accelerated
- Renewable energy innovations flourished

got the infamous murder hornets, the Alaskan zombie fires, the Saharan dust cloud invasion, and the one that still baffles me: the toilet-paper-shortage crisis. Who knew?!

Absolutely no one. And we have no idea what's coming next. It's always been that way, and it's not going to change. Ever.

If we want our teams to avoid the emotional drag that seems to come with uncertainty, we have to somehow help them accept (and even lean into) the constant state of "not knowing."

Uncertainty doesn't have to be something that is feared or dreaded. It just "is." Which brings me to my third point.

GLOBAL ECONOMY TRANSFORMATION (1980S AND 1990S)

Uncertainty

- Foreign imports flooded the market
- Manufacturing moved out of the US
- Jobs and services frequently outsourced
- Many businesses/farms went bankrupt

Opportunity

- Business models shifted to become more globally competitive
- Personal computer sales escalated
- Internet access broadened with the World Wide Web
- NAFTA removed trade barriers
- Longest economic expansion in history ensued

3. UNCERTAINTY HAS AN UPSIDE.

I keep coming back to this question: Why does uncertainty have to be a negative thing?

I'm not talking about the often-tragic events that *create* uncertainty. Wars, tsunamis and pandemics are still firmly in the I'd-rather-have-a-root-canal category. I'm referring to uncertainty itself. Being thrust into a situation filled with unknowns, perhaps as the result of one of those events.

Let's take a closer look at that.

We already know that uncertainty is both stressful and constant. That leaves us with an important choice. Do we allow non-stop uncertainty to overwhelm us with toxic emotions? Or, instead of hoping it doesn't exist or actively dreading its arrival, can we reframe it? What if we could leverage it? Even *embrace* it?

TERRORISM OF 9/11 (2001)

Uncertainty	Opportunity
• Approximately 3,000 people murdered	• Department of Homeland Security created
• Financial markets halted temporarily	• Transportation Security Administration established
• Airplane travel suspended	• Advanced security technology created for airports/public buildings
• War on Terror launched	
• Fear and anger gripped the nation	• Computer backup and recovery systems advanced
	• Global communication/information-sharing deterred terrorism

What if welcoming constant uncertainty could give professionals, leaders and their companies a competitive advantage? Wait, I'll even double down on that.

What if uncertainty is actually something we all *need*—a critical catalyst to transform businesses and take them to the next level?

The answer to both of those questions is absolutely YES. Uncertainty and opportunity are two sides of the same coin.

The Proof

I'm sure you've noticed the graphics at the bottom of the pages throughout this chapter, and I hope you'll spend a few moments to give them a closer look.

For each event featured, you'll find the name of a difficult, uncertainty-producing event in our nation's history,

---

DOT-COM BUBBLE BURST (2000)

Uncertainty

- Stock market crashed
- Nearly $8 trillion in wealth lost
- Inexperienced leaders struggled to respond

Opportunity

- Seasoned leadership became a priority
- Start-ups refocused on viability and profitability
- New rules for stock trading established
- Economy flourished

along with a list of its painful outcomes. A second list, however, highlights some of the greatest advances in medicine, technology, transportation and communication that directly emerged *because of* those disastrous times. Amidst the uncertainty, people were powerfully compelled to identify unique opportunities for addressing unmet needs.

Those who learn how to embrace the upside of uncertainty can use its natural tension to elevate and increase their capacity for problem-solving and innovation.

Consider what that looks like on a business level. Uncertain situations automatically force great leaders to shift into a different mindset. A higher gear where agility is a requirement, not an option. Fast, frequent strategic thinking becomes their lifeline.

"What are our best alternatives, starting right now?"

SUBPRIME MORTGAGE CRISIS (2007)

Uncertainty

- 8.8 million jobs lost
- Housing market tanked
- Banking system began to collapse
- Businesses failed
- Home values plummeted

Opportunity

- Innovative business models developed
- Technology solutions proliferated
- Communication/connection blossomed
- Gig economy emerged

"If there aren't any obvious choices, how can we create some?"

"What are the short- and long-term implications of the decisions we're making?"

"What could go wrong? What's our Plan B?"

"What opportunities might be hidden in the mess?"

I'm not in any way suggesting that we should become stranded in a perpetual "fight-or-flight" mode. However, the uncertainty mindset (and the innate nimbleness that goes with it) could help professionals at any level stay prepared for what we've confirmed is a continuous stream of unknowns coming our way.

Preparation and Perspective

One part of the uncertainty mindset that can give professionals a distinct advantage is a much stronger focus

---

COVID-19 PANDEMIC (2020)

Uncertainty	Opportunity
• Hundreds of thousands died globally	• New hygiene standards established
• Millions of people infected	• Vaccine capabilities dramatically accelerated
• Health care systems severely strained	• New viral treatments developed
• Medical supplies hard to obtain	• Work-from-home technologies proliferated
• No treatments or vaccines existed	• Telemedicine opportunities increased
• Stock market crashed	• E-commerce and delivery services expanded
• Unemployment surged	
• GDP plummeted	

on contingency planning. It's about deliberately invest-ing the time *now* to answer, what would we do if....?

What happens if 80% of our workforce is wiped out during a hurricane? What if there's an explosion at the manufacturing plant that produces the primary materi-als for our product? What if torrential rainfall prevents our trucks from delivering any products to retailers for weeks on end?

Leaders who have rallied their teams to consider the answers to those types of questions can respond more quickly when disaster strikes—and experience less stress in the process. They know without a doubt that uncer-tainty will occur and, at least to some extent, they are pre-pared to deal with it.

Their contingency plans give them the flexibility to work around whatever trauma impacts their business model. And when nothing in those plans prepares them for the crisis at hand, teams are already deeply rooted in the practice of innovative thinking that allows them to "find a way" even when things look completely hopeless.

The uncertainty mindset also provides some valuable perspective, based on what history has taught us: No cri-sis is permanent.

As a business community and a society, we have endured and survived devastating times with far fewer resources and technology than we have today. But the key to maintaining a "this too shall pass" attitude in the middle of a crisis is knowing you have strategies in place to help you and your team make it safely to the other side. Not just surviving, but thriving.

4. UNCERTAINTY DEMANDS A PHASED RESPONSE.

Timing is everything, even if you have some killer strategies ready to deploy. When businesses are suddenly faced with a dramatic shift in the marketplace, leaders need a logical, structured approach—preferably one that doesn't involve remaining completely paralyzed or spinning into a mad frenzy. As I've heard it said, you can eat the elephant only if you do it one bite at a time.

Regardless of the strategies you employ, it's important to understand that your crisis response to uncertainty will be more effective if you approach it in **three different phases**.

Phase One: Stabilize the Business

Whatever role you play within an organization, do what you can to help ensure that the company will remain standing after the dust settles (and it likely will). Your ability to do that may vary, depending on whether you're the CEO, owner, manager or team lead.

For top-level decision-makers, this process might involve implementing budget cuts, issuing a hiring freeze, halting certain projects, negotiating new terms with vendors, or even laying off a percentage of non-essential workers. Not pleasant tasks, to be sure. But if your corporate life is on the line, that kind of belt-tightening is mandatory. Otherwise, game over. For those in mid-level roles, support these initiatives and demonstrate that you understand the need for tough choices.

Phase Two: Grow the Business

Once survival for your company or employer is no longer in question, start searching for hidden opportunities within uncertainty and find creative ways to serve your customers. What can you do right now, in the middle of the crisis, to expand your market share, your revenue or your competitive edge? Think outside the box. Maybe that involves different products, different delivery platforms, or even a different target audience. Look for ways to grow.

Phase Three: Transform the Business

After the uncertainty has died down, analyze the impact of the crisis on your industry, your customers and your competition. How have needs, preferences and resources changed? How can you help your company evolve ahead of the curve to take advantage of that? Be prepared to make these shifts that can create positive transformation.

Professionals who are diligent about moving their companies through these three phases with every bout of uncertainty increase their odds of success, right along with their employers. In some ways, smart leaders and the companies they manage are like diamonds in the rough that emerge from the extreme pressure to become stronger and shinier than ever before.

I should also point out that the progression through these phases isn't always a linear process. Sometimes you have to start back at square one. And I know about that from personal experience.

In 2004, my husband celebrated 20 years in business with his dental practice, located in a mountainous region of western North Carolina. The last place you'd expect to flood, right? Wrong. Hurricane Ivan hit the coast with torrential rainfall, and the local government was slow to release the damn. An eight-foot wall of water crashed into our community's historic district, including my husband's office.

Within 24 hours, all of the patient records, dental equipment and memories were floating in waist-high water. *Enter Phase One.*

We spent the next week trying to put the pieces back together again, cleaning everything up and saving what we could. We found a temporary location for him to practice, and we started the long process of working with the insurance company to get the funds for rebuilding. After the initial shock and the long, difficult days, the light at the end of the tunnel seemed to be just ahead.

Moving toward *Phase Two*, we purchased new equipment, began notifying patients about our temporary location, and started interviewing architects to help us rebuild the original office. Despite the disaster and the inconvenience, this rebuilding effort was going to give my husband the opportunity to upgrade some of his systems and customize the space to better serve his patients. Making lemonade out of lemons, full speed ahead.

Until one week later, when a second hurricane inexplicably hit the coast. The area that never floods was flooded again, boomeranging us right back into *Phase One*.

Once we accepted the reality of the situation (which was particularly tough the second time around), we repeated the clean-up process and revisited our plans for construction. As we made progress toward *Phase Two* again, we decided to use this forced reset as a chance to strengthen our connections with existing clients.

We started interviewing patients and referring doctors to find out what was most important to them in selecting a dentist and what would make them choose one over another. The feedback we got from those interviews was pure gold. In fact, we used it to rewrite the practice's vision, mission, values statement and strategic plan.

Once the office was rebuilt, my husband and his team were more than ready to shift into *Phase Three*. We applied the input we had gathered in *Phase Two* to redesign our patient experience, create a new marketing program, and develop a communication strategy for referrals. Those carefully crafted updates became a true differentiator in the marketplace and the catalyst for significant growth.

The point here is, perseverance is a prerequisite for survival. Sometimes it's one step forward and two steps back. Stay flexible, and don't give up. It's not always a linear progression, but I can guarantee that sticking with it will give you the inside track on longevity.

If your goal is to successfully move yourself and your organization through times of uncertainty, the first step is adopting a different mindset. This is your chance to flip the script. To start thinking about uncertainty from a new angle. To expect it and plan for it. To greet it with strategy, vision and hard work. To model that approach for your co-workers and teams. To use it as a tool for unprecedented innovation and growth.

The chapters ahead will show you exactly how to make that happen.

CHAPTER TWO

Be Relentless About
YOUR VISION

CASWELL-MASSEY FOUNDED 1752

Caswell-Massey is a US-based company that sells personal care products from soaps and fragrances to skincare and men's grooming essentials. Widely considered to be the fourth oldest business in America, the organization has been a favorite across multiple generations.

High-profile clients of Caswell-Massey over the years included New York royalty like the Astors and Vanderbilts, General Armstrong Custer, Greta Garbo, Edgar Allan Poe, Judy Garland, Katharine Hepburn, Joni Mitchell, John Denver, The Rolling Stones, and many US presidents and first ladies, including President John F. Kennedy and Jacqueline Kennedy Onassis.

The company was founded in 1752 in Newport, Rhode Island, by a Scottish-born doctor named William Hunter. It started as an apothecary shop dispensing medicines and selling medical equipment under the name of Dr. Hunter's Dispensary.

Given his swanky Newport location, Hunter ended up with an exclusive clientele who often requested some of the personal care items and essential oils they had seen in Europe. He began stocking those and even customizing them, which attracted prominent early customers including George Washington, Marquis de Lafayette and John Adams. I don't remember any conversations about soap in the Broadway musical *Hamilton*. But if there were, I have a feeling Dr. Hunter might have gotten a sassy hip-hop shout-out.

Rumor also has it that former First Lady Dolley Madison was obsessed with the Caswell-Massey fragrance "White Rose" and even bathed in it. *(Pssssst...Dolley! Less is more.)*

When the American Revolution was in full swing, Dr. Hunter was forced to leave and handed down the company to his assistant—a practice that continued over the next 150 years. Partnerships with businessmen Phillip Caswell in the 1850s and William Massey in 1876 led to the official company name being registered as Caswell-Massey. Through these collaborations, the retail presence grew from two stores to ten.

Despite the company's position at the time as the country's leading perfumer, the Great Depression took its toll. Caswell-Massey was forced to downsize, shrinking to a single retail store to stay in business. The leaders managed to weather that storm and then charted a course for slow, steady growth.

In the 1970s, the company faced stiff competition from retailers like Crabtree & Evelyn. Leaders at that time scrambled to keep up by expanding into shopping malls and, later, drugstore chains—a strategic misstep that put them at odds with their reputation as a high-end, elite brand. The results? Tragically underpriced products and plenty of unsold inventory.

In 1995, as the company was losing $3 million per year, long-time employee Anne Robinson took charge of the organization's 28 stores and 113 employees. Robinson knew that Caswell-Massey's survival depended on a serious reboot. The company needed to get back to its core, recommit to its roots and focus on the original vision. To achieve that, she closed more than half the stores, trimmed down the product line, and let go of 25% of the employees.

By the end of 1998, Robinson and her team had returned the organization to profitability. She assembled a pool of investors to buy the company and began looking at opportunities for expansion. Best of all, Robinson learned from past mistakes. She was adamant that no amount of uncertainty was going to lure the company away from its original vision under her watch.

Today, Caswell-Massey products can still be purchased in high-end retail stores in upscale markets. The company expanded to create licensing agreements with luxury retailers in Italy, Egypt, Saudi Arabia and the Philippines. At the same time, Robinson recognized the need to expand market share by selling a traditional brand with traditional products in a modern way.

She made the decision in October 1999 to try marketing the company's products on QVC, the home shopping network. Eight out of ten products sold out, and she was logging $11,000 in sales per minute during the show.

In addition to being featured on QVC, Caswell-Massey products are now available online. They are promoted through social media to target a younger customer base. The company has also engaged in strategic partnerships for product collaborations with young innovators and institutions, such as the New York Botanical Garden and Yellowstone National Park. The company even found an interesting niche by showcasing its products on reality TV shows.

ANALYZING THE APPROACH

When I studied companies that managed to survive uncertainty for hundreds of years, I found that being relentless about their vision was a universal attribute. Caswell-Massey is a prime example. Not that they did it perfectly all the time. Most companies wander off track at some point in their history. It's extraordinarily easy to get lost in the middle of market challenges and endless obstacles. But when the leaders course-corrected and made the commitment to stay focused on the heart and soul of their corporate existence, they were able to stay afloat when others did not.

All in all, I'd propose that an organization's relationship with its vision is often a strong predictor of its success or failure during times of uncertainty.

When entrepreneurs create business plans for their fledgling companies, the vast majority of them put in the effort to develop a vision statement. *What happens next* determines whether their organizations stand the test of time—or fizzle out quickly.

Some leaders believe writing down the vision means they can check that task off the corporate to-do list and move on to more tangible ones like purchasing office equipment or hiring employees. The corporate GPS that should be navigating the progress of the company gets tucked away into a digital filing cabinet.

The alternative? Successful leaders approach their visions as living, breathing beacons of light that can guide them through the thick fog of uncertainty. They have an unequivocal understanding of what their businesses stand for, and they refuse to waver. That's exactly what Caswell-Massey did.

Strategy #1
Be relentless about your vision. In times of uncertainty, don't get distracted by the chaos. Maintain a laser-sharp focus on your directional goal and know where you want to be when the crisis is over.

LASER-FOCUSING ON THE VISION

Even though Caswell-Massey faced overwhelming uncertainty for nearly three centuries, its leaders repeatedly found a way to return to the original vision. They got crystal-clear on the brand promise and the unchanging pillars upon which the company was founded. Those included these **three tenets**:

1. A respected brand with a rich heritage

With hundreds of years in business, Caswell-Massey is known for its historical significance and powerful reputation. Consumers trust the company to deliver a level of luxury and quality that has satisfied a wide range of discriminating (and famous) customers. The products even served as the official lotions, soaps and fragrances of the White House and the Vice Presidential Mansion throughout the years.

An important part of Caswell-Massey's heritage also involves its tradition of home-grown leadership and independence. The mode of succession for this company frequently involves tapping family members or trusted assistants to continue the legacy. This professional continuity allows the company to maintain its integrity, remain flexible and make agile market responses.

2. An unfailing commitment to quality

The company had immediate credibility from the start since its products were developed by an actual physician. Dr. Hunter's original formulations that used only the purest, most natural ingredients available still exist today, and the company continues to preserve the botanical ingredients like almond, aloe, sandalwood and leather that were part of its innovative beginnings.

In recent years, the company has also taken steps to modernize its image of quality, shifting to sustainable manufacturing and incorporating environmentally responsible packaging.

3. A fierce loyalty to customers

From the beginning, Caswell-Massey was a pioneer in using customer preferences and input for product development. When the company realized customers were reluctant to pay high-end prices for fragrances before smelling them, they created sampler boxes to solve that problem.

They also installed a 12-foot perfume sampling bar in the Manhattan flagship store to invite customers to test their fragrances. The theory? If you try it and like it, you generally buy it. That explains all those employees in Macy's enthusiastically trying to "spritz" you with the latest fragrances as you walk by.

Extensive product personalization is another customer-focused feature associated with Caswell-Massey. The company routinely maintained profiles for some of its top-tier customers, including their favorite scents, colors, hobbies, foods and music.

Based on those profiles, the customers were given variants of their favorite perfumes to sample and provide feedback. The company then refined these scents to develop customized, signature perfumes for each of these upscale users. Sold with a price tag of up to $200 per ounce, these unique creations were bottled as private stock and carefully guarded.

When Caswell-Massey remained focused on the vision, the company thrived. When it didn't, the consequences were severe. That's a valuable lesson for all of us, personally and professionally. Plain and simple, whatever we focus on expands. Whatever gets the most of our time and energy multiples.

For instance, if we focus on all the reasons why uncertainty is not fair and it's causing us to struggle, we'll continue finding more and more reasons why it's terrible. But if we focus instead on all the reasons why we are going to succeed despite uncertainty, we'll find more of those, too.

Let's test that theory.

EXERCISE: THE POWER OF FOCUS

Look around your office, your living room or wherever you are reading this book. Chances are, you'll see a chair, a desk or table, maybe a laptop or a smartphone. Now focus on the color blue and scan the room again.

The blue logos for LinkedIn and Facebook seem to pop off your phone screen. You've looked at the abstract artwork on the wall for months but never really paid any attention to the watercolor shades of royal blue in the upper left corner. The modem has a blue sticker on it. A blue Sharpie on the counter catches your eye. The label on the hand sanitizer bottle has a navy background. Every notepad is striped with pale blue lines.

Nothing in the room is different, but your shift in focus actually changes what you see.

Try it with another color, like black. Same result. Because what we focus on is what we find.

The lesson for us during times of uncertainty is to focus on the opportunities rather than the obstacles. That's not always easy, considering the obstacles probably far outnumber the opportunities. But success isn't logical.

The people who succeed through times of intense struggle don't necessarily have more intelligence, talent, resources or lucky breaks. They just understand that almost everything about the uncertain situation is out of their control—except for one thing: *what they choose to focus on.*

They focus on the reasons they will succeed. On the upside. On the silver linings. Those things expand and push them through each and every struggle. Even better? That intense, expanding focus will help them identify opportunities that align with their vision for the future.

FINDING THE POSITIVE POINT

I once heard a story about a leader who was making plans to take his troop of Scouts on a white-water rafting trip in northern California. It took him more than a year to get the reservations, and the children he was taking had raised money for this adventure all year long.

In the weeks leading up to the trip, that particular area of California was soaked with heavy rains. The white-water rapids that would normally have been rated as a Class 2 of difficulty were now verging on Class 5. The leader understood the additional risks this would pose for his troop and was prepared to cancel the trip.

As you might imagine, the children begged and pleaded with him to reconsider. He spoke at length with the rafting trip guides, who assured him that the excursion was still a possibility *if certain safety precautions were strictly followed.* After those discussions, the leader told the eager kids that the trip was still "on"—with one condition. They would have to agree to participate in a lengthy course on safety before getting in the water.

The guide would normally spend 30–45 minutes covering the rules for the adventure, but the expanded course required three full hours. She described every possible scenario the children might encounter during their experience on the rapidly rushing river.

Here's the interesting part. Even though she invested a significant amount of time discussing the perils of high water, downed trees and other potential debris, she spent twice as long talking about what she called the "positive point."

She explained that getting overly distracted by the elements trying to push them off course would inevitably lead them to steer the raft right into the obstacles. Instead, she told them to *be aware of* the challenges but to keep their focus on exactly where they want the raft to go.

The vision. The goal. The positive point.

Their primary focus would determine the direction of the raft, the journey and the final destination.

Business (and life, for that matter) are the same way. We need a vision—a positive point—that remains ever-present in our strategic minds. When a crisis hits, we can't allow ourselves to get so caught up in the challenges, the setbacks, the bad news and the negative people that we lose sight of the prize. When our leaders and our teams focus relentlessly on the vision, our business will be pulled like a magnet to the precise place we want to go. Yes, vision is that powerful!

HIGHLIGHTING A MODERN EXAMPLE

If someone asked me to name a modern-day company that personifies this strategy, my first response would be Apple. The company has one of the most compelling and driving visions of any business in the world.

Just think about all the ups and downs it has experienced since the company opened its doors in 1976. The massive transformation in technology. The flood of new competitors entering the market. The customer preferences that change almost daily. And yet, as the leaders have expanded the company far beyond computers, they still remain true to their vision.

Tim Cook, Apple's current CEO, defines the organization's vision this way: *"We believe that we are on the face of the earth to make great products, and that's not changing."*

I love that.

It's simple, memorable and easily repeatable. It's also bold and powerful. This vision statement inspires the Apple employees to believe they have unlimited potential. It also stakes a claim and backs it up with a fierce, never-gonna-change declaration. That's relentless commitment to the vision.

APPLYING THE STRATEGY

Now it's time to consider how you can apply this strategy to keep you and your organization strong in times of uncertainty. Your key to survival is having perfect clarity about your identity. Know who you are. Know where you are going—and keep your sights fixed on that destination, no matter how many detours you are forced to take.

For current and future leaders, here are **four steps** to help you implement this first strategy within your organization:

1. Clarify your current vision.

Take a moment to consider how the leaders and employees in your company think about your corporate vision today. Is it like a neon sign leading your teams into the future? Or is it an afterthought metaphorically scribbled on a Post-it Note and stuck in a drawer? Do employees understand it? Does it matter? Do they feel compelled to work toward that positive point every day?

First things first, make sure your vision is distinct from your mission and your values.

Vision	What you believe and hope to achieve
Mission	How you will achieve it
Values	Your guiding principles and your promise to yourself and your company

If you feel like your current vision is lacking the inspiration factor, the answers to the following questions might help you boost the emotional wattage.

- Why are you in business?
- Which customers are you serving?
- What products and services do you produce?
- How do those uniquely meet the needs of your customers better than the alternatives?
- What impact do you want to make on those customers?
- What impact do you want to make on your industry?
- What impact could you make on the world if you achieve your vision? *(socially, technologically, economically, environmentally, politically)*

Another way to get a better handle on your company's relationship with its vision is to gather a diverse group of participants to (literally) paint a picture of that rubber-meets-the-road impact.

EXERCISE: VISION QUEST

This simple yet effective group exercise can help you create a new vision or reconnect with your current one.

Recommended Attendees:

- Group of 6–10
- Executive team, leadership team, peers, colleagues, key staff members

Steps:

- Divide your attendees into three groups.
- Provide each group with a flip chart and markers.
- Ask each group to select a moderator/presenter before starting the exercise.
- Direct each group to brainstorm and draw pictures (or collect digital ones) that represent the vision of success for your company over the next 1–3 years. (Just images; no words or descriptions.)

  - What does success look like for the organization?
  - What does that success look like from the customers' perspective?

- Bring everyone together and ask the three presenters to explain their group's drawings.
- Challenge the full set of attendees to brainstorm together and determine words that would describe each of the images presented.
- List all of those words and phrases on a separate flip chart.
- Identify common words and themes that emerge from the exercise to form the foundation of the vision.
- Encourage group discussion about what the journey toward that vision would look like and what types of uncertainty could get in the way.
- Distill the vision statement with input from the entire group or with guidance from a smaller task force.

2. Analyze your existing operations, products and services.

Do your business operations today fully support your vision? Or have they somehow deviated from the original purpose? As I've mentioned before, it's easy to rationalize away some subtle (or not-so-subtle) shifts during times of uncertainty. But step back and consider if any elements need to be realigned.

One way to help determine whether you are genuinely following your vision is to think about the customer expectations your company has established. What do customers want and need from you? What do they anticipate when purchasing your brand and doing business with you?

Products certainly evolve over time, but the brand (and what it stands for) needs to be rock-solid. If your brand is "wobbly," customers lose trust in you and, worse, lose interest in building a relationship with you.

If you walk into a McDonald's, you're probably not expecting prime rib and gourmet horseradish sauce. That would be super weird, right? You have an expectation for a consistently prepared hamburger that follows general standards across state and (most) national boundaries. People pretty much know what they are getting under the golden arches.

Same thing with going to Tiffany & Co. for some fine jewelry. People shop there for the exceptional service and the little touches that make it feel elegant. It's just not the same if they drop your new diamond necklace into a brown paper bag instead of presenting it in the iconic blue box with the white bow. The Tiffany & Co. experience is part of the purchase.

As you think about your vision and customer expectations, be candid about whether your company is living up to the standards that have been set. Review your operations, procedures, products, services and strategies. Are all of these components intertwined and singularly focused on your positive point?

3. Make a plan to get back on track if you've wandered.

First of all, don't beat yourself up if you discover that your corporate focus has shifted. It happens to every company at some point—even the ones that have been in business for hundreds of years. The key to success is refocusing on your vision and figuring out how to get back on track.

No way to sugarcoat this: That may not be a pleasant task.

Anne Robinson of Caswell-Massey probably wasn't winning any popularity contests when she had to cut product lines and fire employees. But she did what she had to do to save the company, and that meant sacrificing short-term morale for long-term survival. Correcting mistakes can be hard, but great leaders have the fortitude to guide the ship through the roughest of waters.

Perhaps you can already identify areas where your brand has wandered off course. What can you do to refocus on the vision and realign your efforts? How can you communicate the need for that process in a way that gets employees engaged and on board to support the changes?

4. Balance a commitment to the vision with a commitment to innovation.

The vision for your brand should be timeless. With that said, you don't want to run the risk of allowing a classic brand to remain stuck in the past. Your commitment to focusing on the vision needs to occur within the context of an innovative, forward-thinking structure. The core principles remain the same, but everything else should be fluid.

Technology continuously changes your options for production, delivery, promotion, marketing and selling. Customer preferences evolve over time. New markets and target audiences emerge. Fresh opportunities to improve the customer experience will come to light. The key is to avoid getting so carried away with those innovations and evolutions that the foundation of your brand gets lost in the shuffle.

Growth for Caswell-Massey meant scaling beyond the corner-drug-store model of delivery. Manufacturing changed dramatically from the days when Dr. Hunter personally mixed his fragrances and essential oils in the back room. The company experimented with wholesale and retail operations, catalogs, online stores, direct customer sales and strategic partnerships.

The big takeaway here? The back end of the Caswell-Massey business has transformed significantly since 1752. But from the customers' perspective, the soul of the brand remains the same. Whether customers order something from the company online or pick it up at an exclusive boutique, they trust that the products will reflect the luxury, quality and integrity they expect from a time-honored organization.

SEEING THE BIG PICTURE

While we can learn to view uncertainty as a source of opportunity, it also poses an ongoing threat to our focus on the vision. The problem is, the elements that try to divert our attention may arrive in different forms.

For the Scout troop, the dangerous distractions looked like rushing water and unexpected debris. For Caswell-Massey, they were "peer pressure" from competitors using a radically different distribution method. For other businesses, uncertainty may arrive as a recession, a new price-slashing competitor, or the bankruptcy of a critical vendor.

No matter what disguise uncertainty is wearing, this strategy reminds us not to fall for the ruse. Don't get distracted by the chaos. If you want to establish lasting success, remain relentlessly focused on your vision.

CHAPTER THREE

Condition Yourself for
CHANGE

JIM BEAM FOUNDED 1795

Chances are, you're familiar with a brand called Jim Beam. It's one of the top-selling whiskeys in the world, available in more than 195 countries. It started when a German farmer named Jacob Beam moved to Kentucky with his family and all of his belongings—including a copper still.

In 1795, Jacob rolled out the first barrel of corn whiskey made in a style that became known as bourbon. It was, as they say, an instant classic. (Gives new context to the Old-Fashioned, doesn't it?) The company thrived over the years and was passed down through several generations, including to James ("Jim") B. Beam, for whom the company is named today.

Building a brand and producing bourbon for more than 200 years has not been without its challenges. New competitors flooded the marketplace, and customer preferences evolved over time. Across all of those years, the Jim Beam organization found success through its ability to deal with change really well.

In 1820, the leaders of Jim Beam recognized the impact of the Industrial Revolution and saw an opportunity to increase revenue by expanding their reach. In 1854, the company capitalized on the growing network of railroads, moving its distillery closer to the stations for easy access to multi-state distribution.

When Prohibition was made into law in 1920, Jim Beam had been at the helm of the company for 20 years. He was forced to shut down the distillery, but he found a way to support his family by growing citrus in Florida and getting involved with some mining projects. Throughout that entire time, he still protected his family's secret whiskey recipe, while dreaming of the day he could return to his passion of making and selling bourbon.

Jim Beam was 70 years old when Prohibition ended and, despite his age, he quickly led the company to a stunning comeback. He secured three investors and began building a new distillery by hand at record speed. Together with his brothers and his son, they completed the construction and were back in business within 120 days.

While many other distilleries were long gone or declaring bankruptcy, Jim Beam survived because his mindset was conditioned for change. The family leaders bravely faced reality and developed plans to dive back in when their competitors didn't. That was the difference. Not just between success and failure, but between surviving and thriving.

ANALYZING THE APPROACH

In the last chapter, I talked about the importance of being relentlessly focused on our vision—locking in on the goal-aligned opportunities more than the challenges. The story of Jim Beam sheds a little more light on that choice and illuminates the nuances involved.

When we're experiencing uncertainty, we can't pretend the challenges don't exist or simply wish them away. We have to be prepared to operate in the realm of reality.

Let's explore that.

Many things that impact our success in business and in life are completely outside of our control. We can be sailing along smoothly, handling the garden-variety brand of uncertainty in our lives, and then—*bam!*—we suddenly crash into heavy-duty, industrial-strength uncertainty. I'm talking about major disruptions. Natural disasters. Recession. Bankruptcy. Extended supply chain disruptions. Disease. Liability lawsuits.

The truth is, our well-made plans can and will be disrupted by uncertainty-producing events. Sooner or later. And probably more than once. In the process of writing this book, I studied how leaders historically react to these situations, and I discovered several predictable responses.

For some, uncertainty prompts panic, chaos and a wild adrenaline rush of frenzied action. For others, they greet uncertainty with a sense of cheery denial: *"Everything's fine. Let's just keep doing what we're doing, and the situation will resolve itself."*

Neither of those approaches is particularly helpful, personally or professionally.

Leaders with companies that outlast their competition have found a better strategy to deal with the very-certain occurrence of uncertain events. The key? They accept reality, even when it is uncomfortable and messy. More importantly, they prepare for it in advance. They scan the horizon for glimmers of light in the darkness, and they proceed with confidence while knowing beyond a shadow of a doubt that the sun will rise again.

Think about Jim Beam planting orange trees to put food on the table for his family, all while envisioning the design for a state-of-the-art distillery that would someday make his bourbon a household name.

> **Strategy #2**
> **Condition yourself for change and anticipate the next wave of uncertainty. When it hits, accept reality while proactively searching for new opportunities.**

EMBRACING THE SUCK

One way to think about this strategy might be to say, "keep calm and carry on." (Hey, maybe they should put that slogan on a T-shirt!) But uncertainty for current and future leaders can be brutal, and it might be more impactful to describe it in terms that capture the "real" in the reality.

Embrace the suck. There's a concept, right?

Time for the cold, hard facts. When uncertainty is staring you in the face, you can't succeed unless you first accept it, understand it and actually embrace the fact that there's no other way out. You just have to walk through it. No panic, no denial. Just calm resolve and steady actions. Yep, embrace the suck.

I actually learned that phrase from studying the military, where it is used as a reminder to view challenges as opportunities to grow and expand rather than insurmountable roadblocks.

During the Vietnam War, several thousand American soldiers were captured by the North Vietnamese and held as prisoners of war (POWs). They were confined in tiny cells where they were tortured, beaten and starved. Some were even subjected to years in solitary confinement with no human contact whatsoever. At the end of the war, 591 soldiers returned home. Let that sink in: Only 591 survived while all the others died.

One of those survivors was Commander James Stockdale, now a Medal of Honor recipient. For more than seven years, he was repeatedly tortured as a POW. When Stockdale talked about the nightmare experience of the war years later, he was sometimes asked to describe his fellow soldiers who *had not* made it out of the camps. His response was surprising. *"That's easy,"* he said. *"It was the optimists."*

He explained that the glass-half-full people were consumed with envisioning a happy ending that never materialized. *("We'll be home by Christmas!")* It destroyed them from the inside out.

Stockdale, on the other hand, opted to embrace the suck:

> "You must never confuse faith that you will prevail in the end—which you can never afford to lose—with the discipline to confront the most

brutal facts of your current reality, whatever they might be."

That nugget of wisdom is now known as the Stockdale Paradox, and it's the true definition of embracing your reality to achieve success. It's a blend of keeping the faith, maintaining a strong mindset, *and* boldly accepting the harsh situation you've landed in.

For decision-makers at any level, this is like a big dose of strategic planning reality. We can't change the past; we can control only what happens from this moment going forward. These are the cards we've been dealt. But it's our move, and our only choice is to play the hand we've got.

When uncertainty is staring us down, we need to get real and get moving with a viable plan to recover and come back stronger.

MOVING PAST OUR OWN PERCEPTIONS

Thanks to some of my own recent experiences, this strategy really resonates with me.

When the COVID-19 virus prompted shut-downs that paralyzed many businesses in 2020, I volunteered to partner with local chambers of commerce and the SCORE organization. We joined forces to counsel their members and clients (many of them small business owners) who were trying desperately to keep their companies from going under.

As I began working with these entrepreneurs, I assumed their biggest challenge would be figuring out how to adjust their business models to sell their products/services remotely and deliver them in a healthy, CDC-approved manner.

Oh boy, was I wrong.

What was the top obstacle for the vast majority of them? *Accepting reality.* They simply didn't want to face the fact that a pandemic had turned the world upside down. Not their fault. But definitely their problem. These leaders were missing the point by viewing reality through their own less-than-accurate lenses.

One shop owner I met was extremely optimistic. She declared with confidence that she'd be open for business again in two weeks when things were "back to normal." Even though walk-in traffic at her store was down by 95%, she wasn't interested in developing a long-term plan. She firmly believed she wouldn't need it.

On the flip side, one gentleman who owned a small manufacturing company was completely distraught and highly emotional about the economic challenges. When he realized he wouldn't be able to purchase the supplies he needed from his usual vendors in Taiwan and Vietnam, he was ready to give up. Right then. He wanted to declare bankruptcy before he had even depleted his current inventory.

Both individuals—the optimist and the pessimist—were trapped in a pattern of thinking that paralyzed them. When we start with a skewed view of reality, our response is destined to fail.

So what happens when companies ignore reality (or rely on their own perceptions of it) and fail to embrace the suck? Ask the former leaders at Borders. They refused to believe that e-books and online retailers like Amazon would dominate the market, which prompted them to file for bankruptcy in 2011.

Forget about whether you personally prefer to view the world as the glass half-full or half-empty. *See it as it is.* Be prepared for what you might find. And make sure you're in the best possible shape to handle whatever that looks like.

GETTING IN SHAPE

Preparing to survive corporate uncertainty isn't all that different from world-class runners preparing for a marathon.

They make a commitment to work hard, not for just a few days, but for the long haul. They are comfortable with the effort it takes to get in shape and maintain that level of conditioning. They practice handling the challenges that always come with the territory—difficult terrain, injuries, inclement weather. When the race day arrives, they know it won't be easy, but they know they can do it. They've done it before.

The lesson for current and future leaders is to follow that lead. Uncertainty conditioning is like a muscle. The more we talk about change, think about change and pre-pare for change, the stronger our muscles will be. When we're conditioned for adversity, we can easily adapt and continue instead of burying our heads in the sand and ignoring it. And when we get really good at "riding the wave" of change, we can also search for new opportunities while we're navigating the unknown.

HIGHLIGHTING A MODERN EXAMPLE

One company that has successfully turned uncertainty into a strategic advantage—using change rather than fearing it—is Netflix. Since its inception in 1998, the business has morphed and changed almost constantly.

This DVD rental and sales company started by taking on competitor Blockbuster Video. They knew that Blockbuster's customers were annoyed by time limits and late fees involved with renting movies from the neighborhood retail location. Netflix wanted to make it more convenient, offering a mail-based system that provided much more flexibility.

In the late 1990s, customers began expressing interest in having more viewing options and greater variety in their movie choices. Netflix responded with an innovative program in 1999, adding a subscription service that allowed customers to become members and rent unlimited DVDs for a flat monthly rate.

The next year, the company augmented the subscription model to make recommendations for movies and shows that members might enjoy, based on their viewing history. That popular addition helped to keep them one step ahead of their competitors.

Netflix went public in 2002 with relatively steady growth, while monitoring the market closely. What did they find? Customers weren't wild about having to wait for DVDs to come in the mail. They wanted to be able to watch their choice of movies whenever they wanted.

In 2007, Netflix introduced its streaming service that put the company on the map in a really big way. Its next innovation came in 2016. Netflix started creating its own content, once again leading the market in a shift that would become commonplace for the industry.

The company's continued success stems from its innate connection with its customers and the ability to stay on the front edge of understanding their wants and needs. More importantly, the organization isn't afraid of change and doesn't hesitate to respond. By staying nimble and flexible, Netflix has been able to maintain an impressive edge.

When teams stop fighting change and learn to use it as an advantage, industry leadership often follows.

APPLYING THE STRATEGY

Now it's your turn. How well are you conditioned to deal with uncertainty? Do you perceive every bump in the business road as a red-alert disaster? Or do you sport the rose-colored glasses 24/7, 365? Are you in shape and prepared for whatever is coming next?

For professionals who want to apply this strategy toward achieving success within their organizations, here are **three steps** that may be helpful:

1. Evaluate your existing level of uncertainty conditioning.

Start by thinking about your current reality, whether you are the CEO or a mid-level manager. Is your business booming? Or are you concerned about the health of the organization? How do you feel about that as a leader or an employee?

When faced with uncertainty, what is your typical response? Are you surprised and frustrated by it, every single time? Are you resolved and ready with a game plan to tackle the challenges? Do you allow your inner opti-mist or pessimist to block out the reality of the situation?

Be brutally honest about whether you have a natural tendency to perceive challenges through a tinted lens.

2. Learn how to effectively frame a challenge or crisis.

In many cases, it's hard for professionals (and people, in general) to create a plan to push through uncertainty until they get the fears out of their heads and onto paper. If you are in that stage (or anticipate being there), this brainstorming exercise can help you capture the depth and breadth of the problem at hand within your organization.

EXERCISE: REALITY CHECK

Participants: Individual leaders and/or entire teams

a. **Define the nature and scope of a crisis situation or challenge you are facing (or expect to face in the future).** Write down as much detail as you can in a one-page summary that includes a concise statement of the problem, the contributing factors and parameters, the business functions affected, and the implications (short- and long-term). To guide your discussion, consider the impact on the following areas:

Branding & communication	Resource allocation
Business growth	Risk management

Customer acquisition & retention	Sales & marketing
Financial & economic issues	Strategic vision
Globalization	Systems, processes & procedures
Lead generation	Talent acquisition & retention
Leadership succession	Technology shifts
Market competition	Training & development
Product/service innovation	Workplace culture & diversity
Regulatory requirements	Other

b.   What is the best-case scenario for the outcome of this crisis/challenge?

c.   What is the worst-case scenario for the outcome of this crisis/challenge?

d.   What is the realistic expectation for the outcome (which is probably somewhere in the middle)?

e.   Which contributing factors are fixed and which ones can you control? Examples might include:

Things You Can't Control

- Competitors moving into your space
- Tax impact from your country's debt
- Supplier price hikes
- New industry regulations
- Natural disasters and pandemics

Things You Can Control

- Business strategy adjustments
- Customer communications *(how well and how often)*
- Value proposition updates
- Employee engagement
- Culture of innovation

f. **How much time and energy are you spending (or are you likely to spend) on factors beyond your control?** What progress could you make if you focus on what you *can* control while simply staying mindful of what you *can't*?

g. **Given all of these factors, what specifically can you do RIGHT NOW to accept the reality of the situation, take control of the next steps, and prepare for whatever outcome emerges?**

Writing down this information succinctly often helps reality sink in. And once you've done that, you may find it easier to formulate a plan to push through the struggles and chart a productive course toward the future.

I recently used this exercise with one of my clients who owns and operates an events business. She earns all of her annual revenue from planning parties and events, as well as supplying the food and lodging for attendees. Many of her customers are involved with games and tournaments for soccer, cheerleading and basketball.

When COVID-19 hit in early 2020, everything on her calendar was postponed. Group events, group trips, group meals. All of it.

Her first inclination was to spring into action and find a way to stay in business. She downsized her staff and contacted her clients personally in a desperate bid to reschedule or restructure some of the high-dollar bookings. She frantically ordered masks and gloves. She researched safe alternatives to hold large gatherings during a pandemic.

Then she hit a wall. She couldn't sleep. She couldn't function. She was consumed with worry about how long the pandemic would last and whether her comeback would be dashed by the treacherous "second wave" that the doctors warned about. How would she survive if the virus lingered and events weren't just postponed but canceled?

In a matter of a week, she went from optimist to pessimist. She felt like the struggle was starting to defeat her, and it was threatening to take her business down at the same time. She reached out to me for advice.

After we discussed the unfathomable situation she was facing, I knew she needed to sit down and work through this Reality Check exercise. We went through the questions together, and then I encouraged her to do it again with her staff. The results were extremely powerful.

The team emerged from the conversation with a concrete list of opportunities, challenges, strengths and threats. After dividing the list into two categories—what they could control and what they couldn't—an action plan started to emerge. Admittedly, there were plenty of fixed variables, but concentrating on the others (as small as they might have been) made a big difference. In the business and in their morale.

The main point? When she and her team members were able to articulate the exact problem and identify which factors they could control, they were able to release their fears (or at least quiet them) and envision the seeds of a solution. They moved from being stuck to being free to identify possibilities for the future—one that looked vastly different than they anticipated on New Year's Day but one in which they remained in business. The resilience bubbled up within them, and they accepted the challenge.

3. Implement a plan to maintain your conditioning.

Once you and your team see the value of anticipating and framing challenges, it's time to make that part of your ongoing process. So how do you remain conditioned for change over the long haul? For starters, it takes a tool and a plan. It doesn't just happen without intentional effort.

One approach I recommend for my clients is called the SKEPTIC tool. And just for reference, that's a handy acronym. Nothing skeptical about how it works!

EXERCISE: SKEPTIC TOOL

Participants: Leaders, colleagues, peers and/or teams

This exercise helps teams to weave "uncertainty training" into their regular business processes. The goal should be for teams or peers to meet together once a month and actively brainstorm in these seven areas for 30–60 minutes.

The components of the SKEPTIC tool include the following:

Society	What changes do you see occurring in society that could impact the company or its products/services?
Competition (K)	How do you see the competition changing, for better or worse?
Economy	What economic trends are occurring? How long will they last? And how will they affect the business?
Politics	How are political changes impacting your business, your customers, your employees and your vendors?
Technology	How are changes in technology transforming your ability to produce/sell/ deliver products and communicate with your customers?
Industry	What industry changes do you need to be monitoring? What are the potential implications for your business?
Customers	Are customer needs and preferences shifting? Do you have opportunities to meet those needs in a unique way and demonstrate leadership?

My clients have gotten optimal results with this tool when they approach it in two rounds of discussions. In the first, they encourage free-flowing idea generation with no "edits" or qualifiers. The second round focuses more on identifying conclusions and solutions.

Best of all, this exercise helps teams answer some critical questions. What, if anything, on this list do we need to be paying attention to? Are there any changes we need to worry about right now? Do we see any opportunities that require our immediate action? By taking the time to address these issues every 30 days, you can keep your team in shape and fully anticipating whatever form of uncertainty lies ahead.

Speaking of anticipation... I realize that a month can fly by while teams are working on deadlines and trying to meet and exceed goals. I can guarantee that your team members involved with this ongoing exercise will eventually say, *"Didn't we just do that? Nothing's really changed, so let's skip it for now."*

Refuse to give in.

Olympic swimmers don't take a month off, even if they just swam 20 miles yesterday. It's that commitment to constant monitoring of the business environment that allows organizations to detect the first signs of uncertainty and capitalize on them. Make it fun. Challenge your team to find new things on the horizon. By infusing that kind of tone, you'll be embedding this process into the fabric of your mental conditioning. And trust me, you'll reap the rewards.

One of my clients in the health care industry credits this tool with much of their company's success. In the past 12 months, this exercise allowed them to anticipate uncertainty and take advantage of multiple opportunities that translated into bottom-line impact.

In their SKEPTIC discussions about competitors, the group identified several that were struggling in markets they had been trying to enter for years. This opened up a number of merger and acquisition options that ultimately increased their market share and revenue.

During conversations about the economy, the team analyzed how many other health care organizations were having to downsize or furlough employees. Leaders decided to use that situation as an opportunity to scoop up some really strong talent, while letting go of those who hadn't been pulling their weight.

Finally, the SKEPTIC exercise helped the organization reverse a year-long decision to shut down a particular business line. While that choice made sense months before, the brainstorming session uncovered significant new shifts within the industry. Keeping the business line intact allowed the company to pursue some brand-new markets.

SEEING THE BIG PICTURE

Being conditioned for change takes a continued investment of time and energy, but it gives savvy professionals the strength to keep going when others might get derailed.

On the day Prohibition was struck down, then-senior-citizen Jim Beam saw his chance and was ready to jump back into the bourbon game. When the CEO of Netflix was learning about the possibilities of streaming (while still mailing DVDs to customers), he had the wisdom to suggest tossing out the old business model.

Conditioning and preparation allow current and future leaders to see opportunities when everyone else is scrambling to make sense of the uncertainty. They see the reality, but they guide their teams to remain versatile, courageous and successful. That's exactly what defines these companies as long-term survivors with lasting success.

CHAPTER FOUR

Get Creative with
COLLABORATION

BAKER'S CHOCOLATE FOUNDED 1765

In late 1764, a young Irish immigrant named John Hannon was unemployed, but he had a big dream. A *sweet* dream, if you will.

Before he arrived in the Boston area, he spent some time in London and learned a special technique for making chocolate. He had a feeling the unique product could be quite popular on this side of the pond, but he didn't have the money or facilities to translate that knowledge into a business. And besides, he had bills to pay.

Hannon would have to get really creative to pursue his dream—or he'd end up filling out a job application at the 1700s equivalent of McDonald's. His response to the uncertainty? Collaboration.

First, Hannon pitched his idea to a general store owner named James Baker, who saw great potential in his vision and was willing to put up the financial support. Then things got interesting.

Hannon approached the owners of a local saw mill that was powered by the water in the Neponset River. He proposed sharing a small space in their mill and using their water power to grind his chocolate. The records don't indicate whether he paid his rent in cash or dessert but, either way, this unlikely partnership worked quite well.

Thanks to the collaboration, Hannon created a successful business serving the Milton and Dorchester areas of Massachusetts.

When the saw mill was sold three years later, Hannon moved to Boston, where he was quickly in search of a new collaborative partner. He introduced himself to the owner of a fulling mill there and secured the same arrangement.

In 1780, after Hannon passed away, original financier James Baker bought the company from Hannon's widow, shut down his general store and pursued the chocolate business full-time. From that point on, his products were branded as "Baker's Chocolate." Baker expanded the business to operate in a number of different mills, bartering with local merchants and trading supplies for ground cocoa.

The company was passed down through the family for a number of generations, but one thing remained the same. Leaders at Baker's Chocolate consistently found success by forging relationships with other businesses that had the resources they needed.

Today the company is owned by Kraft Heinz—oddly enough, another collaborative corporation—and it is considered one of the largest chocolate brands in America.

ANALYZING THE APPROACH

John Hannon had an extraordinary vision and all the right skills to create an iconic brand, but he couldn't possibly make it happen by himself. The lesson for us? Some challenges are too overwhelming for one person, one leader, one company or even one industry to handle on their own. They require teamwork.

When uncertainty delivers insurmountable challenges, we have to find the right partners to get the job done. Sometimes that collaboration involves joining forces with a completely unexpected source—think chocolate making and lumber production. Other times, it means finding the humility to team up with a fierce competitor.

Winston Churchill, one of my personal idols, provided us with a textbook example of how this works. During World War II, Churchill was the prime minister of the United Kingdom and recognized a serious problem. As much as he hated to admit it, he knew his country needed help to weather the storms of battle. The United

Kingdom didn't have the size, strength or resources to defeat the Axis alliance of Germany, Japan and Italy.

He first convinced the president of the United States, Franklin Delano Roosevelt, to support and join the British troops in their fight. Then came the really tough part. He knew he had to forge an alliance with the Soviet Union—a daunting adversary since 1917. These countries were polar opposites in every way that mattered. Economically. Politically. Religiously. And yet, Churchill boarded a plane to extend the proverbial olive branch to Joseph Stalin, the Soviet dictator.

I can only imagine what was going through his mind at the time.

"I really don't like this guy or anything he stands for. He's despicable. We can't agree on the time of day. But my best chance to help the UK survive involves persuading him to work with us toward a common goal. Not my first choice, but...desperate times. Let's go."

Churchill saw that his only path to success involved transforming competition into collaboration. His instincts were spot-on. Just think where we might be today without his courage and insight!

Assuming your competitors haven't starved, imprisoned or murdered thousands of people, proposing a collaborative effort as a tool for survival will likely be a little easier than teaming up with a brutal dictator. How's that for perspective?

> ### _Strategy #3_
>
> **_Get creative with collaboration during times of extreme uncertainty, even if it means working with a competitor. The synergy you produce can give both parties a better chance at survival._**

DESIGNING WIN-WIN PARTNERSHIPS

A number of my clients have implemented this strategy with great results, and I'm always fascinated by the examples of their innovative collaboration.

One that immediately comes to mind is a health care business that had been experiencing tremendous, steady growth. Then the leaders started to notice a drop in their rate for bringing in new customers.

The company's expansion had always been fueled by its emphasis on building personal relationships. Unfortunately, they discovered that using an in-person sales model was being perceived as old-fashioned. Customers were becoming increasingly sophisticated and expected a sales experience that was more advanced and digitally enabled.

As the executive team explored options to rectify the problem, a brilliant opportunity for collaboration emerged.

A local IT firm that started in 2000 had been extremely successful with a virtual sales model, but the industry it had been serving was dying out. The leaders were in search of a new market niche.

When these two organizations teamed up, it was the ultimate win-win situation. My client's company helped the IT firm break into the lucrative health care market. Likewise, the IT firm helped the health care business learn how to sell virtually and project the technological sophistication that customers were craving.

Collaboration gave both companies the edge they needed to move past significant challenges with great success.

HIGHLIGHTING A MODERN EXAMPLE

Supermarket giant ALDI was designated as an essential business during the initial COVID-19 lockdown in the spring of 2020. Demand for groceries spiked as people were forced to primarily eat at home during the quarantine period. On the surface, that sounds like great news for ALDI, but the truth was more complicated.

To accommodate CDC guidelines about limiting crowd sizes, the leaders at ALDI had to extend their store hours to give all of their customers a chance to get the groceries they needed. That presented a real staffing shortage.

Many employees with pre-existing conditions or other problematic circumstances chose not to work at that time because of the increased health risks. ALDI managers desperately needed more employees, and they recognized that keeping those workers safe would a pivotal part of their survival.

The opposite problem was happening at McDonald's. While their restaurants were also considered essential businesses, dining service was limited to the drive-through lanes. Suddenly, every McDonald's restaurant had a surplus of workers on the edge of filing for unemployment.

Collaboration saved the day.

ALDI and McDonald's created an unusual partnership that allowed the hamburger chain's surplus employees to temporarily work at ALDI stores. Through this collaborative effort, McDonald's protected its own people from certain layoffs while removing them from the payroll for a limited time when revenue hit rock-bottom. ALDI got access to a large pool of trained workers with customer-service experience to help cover the extended-hour shifts throughout their stores.

McDonald's and ALDI may not be direct competitors in the strictest sense, but they do compete for consumers' dollars to feed their families. By shifting gears and teaming up during a pandemic, these companies both found solutions to their problems. Communities were better served, workers were provided with an employment safety net, and businesses facing a crisis found a creative way through a difficult time.

APPLYING THE STRATEGY

Has uncertainty dealt you or your business a blow so mighty that you fear there's no coming back? Before you give up or give in, pause to think strategically about what it would take to survive. I'm not referring to a huge cash infusion, although those are always helpful. I'm talking about identifying the granular "survival needs" that come to light only with hyper-creative, way-outside-the-box thinking.

The **four steps** that follow can help you walk through that process as a current or future business leader:

1. Identify and analyze the top challenges you are facing.

Revisit the SKEPTIC tool from the previous chapter, and pinpoint the top three challenges that are creating smack-down-level uncertainty for your business right now. The categories for discussion include Society, Competition, Economy, Politics, Technology, Industry and Customers.

How much do you really know about each of these challenges? Do the research. Make sure you're fully informed about the characteristics, parameters, related trends and forecasts, anticipated timelines, expert opinions and competitive responses. If you're going to tackle these foes, you have to know exactly what you are up against.

2. Pinpoint the specific implications.

Correlate the external challenges of uncertainty with the internal impact on your department or organization. What areas of your business are being affected and what are the implications, short-term and long-term?

Scarce product materials	Changing industry standards
Reduced product quality	Shrinking margins
Customer service lapses	Not enough qualified talent
Increased competition	High employee turnover
Pricing pressures	Corporate image erosion
Decreased sales	Other
Customer attrition	
Outdated technology	
Poor client communication	

1. Make a targeted list of what you would need to minimize (or eliminate) this negative impact.

a. What resources would allow the business to control the damage or negative outcomes?

b. What skill sets or talents could help the company offset and overcome the uncertainty?

c. What contacts and relationships would add significant value as you work through the challenges?

d. What resources would give you the bandwidth to identify and pursue opportunities in the midst of this uncertainty?

2. Brainstorm to find potential partners who could provide the things you need to get through the crisis.

Let go of the attitude that you should be able to solve your own problems independently and supply all of the necessary resources. During times of intense uncertainty, that's not realistic. Especially when time is critical.

Discard the pride associated with self-sufficiency, and start searching for more innovative answers.

Who do you know with the capabilities, resources, contacts or knowledge base that you need right now to be successful despite uncertainty? Look beyond the obvious. Maybe that's a vendor, a competitor, a customer, or a company that has absolutely no connection what-soever to your industry. Is there an opportunity for a win-win collaboration? What value could you or your business provide for them? Can you envision a team effort?

Finding the right partner will probably require a deeper level of discussion than you'll have with a one-hour meeting in the conference room, even if all of you are hopped up on strong coffee and chocolate dough-nuts. This involves some serious envelope-pushing.

If you identify some genuine contenders, make a plan to reach out to those organizations and explore the opportunities for a collaborative venture. Highlight the mutually beneficial aspects of the potential partner-ship. The worst they can say is no, and you haven't lost anything.

One of my clients who found success by using this strategy was selling technology to restaurants and bars. When the pandemic hit in 2020, her customers were struggling to pay the bills, so tech upgrades were com-pletely off the table.

She needed a new plan right away or she was facing a certain dead-end. Unfortunately, penetrating a new mar-ket not only requires a major financial investment but also years of hard work to make contacts and build a rep-utation among a fresh set of customers.

She didn't have the luxury of time.

I encouraged her to work through these steps in search of a solution that didn't involve liquidating her business.

After a great deal of research and brainstorming, she uncovered some surprising pockets of opportunity in the manufacturing industry. She felt confident that her products could be targeted to resolve some of the issues being faced by many companies in that space.

As a first step, she reached out to a well-known industry vendor who provided paper products to manufacturers and asked for an informational meeting. She wanted to learn more about what they did and how they served their manufacturing clients. Honestly, she was a bit surprised that they agreed to meet with her.

The appointment went well, and it confirmed her research about the huge potential and rapid growth of the manufacturing sector. On the other hand, she learned that this vendor was increasingly concerned about becoming too dependent on manufacturing. They viewed their lack of diversification as a disadvantage.

That conversation sparked a collaborative, highly profitable partnership that has delivered mutual benefits for both companies.

They decided to pool their resources and their contacts to identify potential leads in other industries. They exchanged information about which products and services might be a good fit for new customers, and they started sharing referrals. When one of them got a new client, they would open the door to bring in the other partner.

Without the extreme uncertainty of a pandemic that prompted this connection, these companies might never have crossed paths. Based on the results, I have a feeling that both organizations will continue this prosperous partnership for many years to come.

SEEING THE BIG PICTURE

Sometimes uncertainty doesn't just change the rules; it obliterates the playing field. Survival, rather than success, becomes the primary goal. The only way out could involve teaming up with your biggest competitor. Or one of your best customers. Or a trusted vendor. Or even an organization you've only read about in *The Wall Street Journal*.

Your creativity is the only limit.

If you uncover an opportunity for collaboration that would add value for both parties, don't write it off as an insane "Hail Mary" pass in the last seconds of a losing game. Make the contact, and make your case. After all, John Hannon approached the owners of a saw mill about making chocolate in their lumber factory. That bold move led to the creation of a centuries-old brand with timeless appeal.

Collaboration made it possible.

CHAPTER FIVE

Be Clear About Your
CORE VALUES

KING ARTHUR BAKING COMPANY FOUNDED 1790

An enterprising gentleman named Henry Wood started a business in 1790, importing and distributing English-milled flour to bakers in Boston, Massachusetts. With this venture, he created the first flour company in America, as well as the first food company in New England. By the 1820s, Wood was able to stop importing his raw materials when he tapped into the new, plentiful supply of American-grown wheat.

Even as competition in the flour market began to heat up, the high-quality products from Henry Wood & Company became a trusted and preferred kitchen staple.

In 1895, the Industrial Revolution transformed the flour industry with the invention of the roller mill. These mills automated and accelerated the process of breaking up the grain before it was ground into flour. However, there were some downsides: less control over quality and consistency. Despite the production advantages available from this "new technology," the leaders at Henry Wood & Company weren't willing to accept that trade-off. No roller mills for them.

I'm sure their competitors were thrilled to hear about that decision.

"They must be crazy! We've got the capability to make more flour faster and sell it for less. Why wouldn't they jump on that bandwagon? Those fools will be out of business before the end of the year!"

Little did they know, the executive team at Henry Wood & Company decided from day one that quality was a hill they were willing to die on.

Shortly after that, one of the business owners attended a performance of *King Arthur and the Knights of the Round Table*. He was intrigued by the unique collection of characteristics attributed to these regal knights: "purity, loyalty, honesty, superior strength, and a dedication to a higher purpose." That set of values really resonated with him. In fact, the more he thought about it, those values also seemed to capture the spirit behind his flour company.

From the very beginning, the organization's leaders were committed to high standards with fair pricing and a quality guarantee with every purchase. They were known for having honest salesmen with unwavering integrity. And they firmly believed that customers would pay a little more to get a premium product that was reliably consistent and pure. No cutting corners.

While most people wouldn't have immediately drawn parallels between the Knights of the Round Table and a flour company, the core values were surprisingly similar.

Want to take a wild guess about the first topic of discussion at the next staff meeting in 1896? Name change! That's how King Arthur Flour (and the King Arthur Flour Company) came into existence.

As the company's popularity blossomed, King Arthur Flour became an American classic. It was the ingredient bakers relied on as they introduced the first apple pie, the first sourdough bread, the first chocolate chip cookie and the first take-out pizza.

With that said, being in business for more than two centuries meant that the King Arthur Flour Company faced its fair share of challenges and serious encounters with uncertainty. Shifting government regulations. Wars. Wheat shortages. Technology that went far beyond the roller mills. But through it all, company leaders could perfectly articulate who they were as a company and what they sold.

When competitors tried to lure customers away with cheaper prices, King Arthur Flour never flinched. They knew that quality mattered in the end. Period. They stuck to their core values, and customers rewarded them with fierce loyalty.

Even better? Those core values gave real purpose to the employees at King Arthur Flour. They understood the company's true identity, and they felt invested in projecting those qualities as they did their jobs. That understanding united them along the path they took to reach a common goal.

In some ways, core values became the metaphorical team cheer that encouraged everyone at King Arthur Flour to participate in supporting the company. Engagement skyrocketed. Accountability soared. And the inevitable results showed up in market share and revenue.

We can actually see the impact of that core-values focus at King Arthur Flour today.

The company—rebranded in 2020 as King Arthur Baking Company to better reflect its extensive product line and baking tools—is now 100% employee owned and was recently named the Employee Stock Ownership Plan (ESOP) company of the year. Plus, as a certified B Corporation, it has been recognized as a business that meets the highest standards of social and environmental performance, public transparency, and legal accountability to balance profit and purpose. Its bylaws reflect a commitment to all stakeholders, including the community and the environment.

Centuries of uncertainty were no match for a flour company named after some legendary knights. Without a doubt, the key ingredient that allowed King Arthur Baking Company to continuously rise up and achieve unparalleled success was an unswerving dedication to core values.

ANALYZING THE APPROACH

Most top executives would agree on this statement: decision-making becomes exponentially harder during times of uncertainty. The number of unknowns in the equations can be absolutely mind-boggling. In the face of that, some decision-makers suffer from "analysis paralysis," simply unable to respond or choose a direction. Others succumb to "shiny object syndrome" and start grabbing at any idea that comes along, desperate for a possible lifeline.

So what's the secret to making good decisions in the midst of bad situations? How can current and future leaders discern which ideas to avoid and which ones to pursue? It all comes back to core values. When companies know what they stand for, they can use those values as a tool to help them move forward.

That's exactly how King Arthur Flour Company navigated uncertainty, over and over again. Was it tempting to adopt the slick efficiencies of the new roller mill technology? I'm quite certain it was. But the owners refused to sacrifice quality. That core value was their guiding light. Their North Star. It became the true litmus test to determine whether a decision was right or wrong for the company.

As I researched the characteristics of organizations that survived uncertainty for hundreds of years, a commitment to core values was undeniably a recurring theme. Companies that had their sights firmly set on long-term success considered those values to be a mandatory component.

The lesson for all of us? Our core values, in essence, create the identity of our brands. They represent a promise we make to our customers, and they define a purpose that inspires our colleagues and employees. Powerful stuff, huh? Best of all, a dedication to core values can provide organizations with some level of immunity from the deadly effects of outrageous uncertainty.

Strategy #4
Be clear about your core values and commit to upholding them consistently. Don't allow uncertainty to throw you off course.

PROVIDING PURPOSE FOR EMPLOYEES

Sometimes it's easier to think about the external impact on customers that occurs when companies remain true to their core values. The less obvious but equally important impact is internal. Employees who work for organizations with well-defined, ever-present core values tend to have a much stronger sense of purpose—a focused drive that accelerates their productivity and performance.

Plenty of scientific studies have proven that fact, but thought leader and author Simon Sinek boiled the idea down to a single, cohesive point:

> "If you go to work in a purpose-driven organization, you are a happier person...and you will go home happier."

I can probably guess what you're thinking. When leaders identify the bottom-line boosting attributes they want in their employees, happiness might seem like a frivolous choice. But, according to research, they would be flat-out wrong.

Happy, purpose-focused employees—those who understand and project the core values—are more engaged, more loyal to their companies, more willing to go the extra mile to serve customers, and more invested in helping the organization succeed.

You can bet that those traits multiplied by the total number of employees produces a radically profitable synergy. Internally and externally, an unchanging focus on core values gives companies the incredible staying power they need to survive, succeed, grow and prosper. But it doesn't just happen on its own. The responsibility for keeping that focus as a top priority falls on the organization's current and future leaders.

HIGHLIGHTING A MODERN EXAMPLE

Chick-fil-A is one of the best examples of a company that lives and breathes its core values. This fast-food restaurant chain that specializes in chicken sandwiches is flourishing because of its full and complete alignment with the company values.

You'd like to hear more? My pleasure! (That response should make sense if you've eaten at a Chick-fil-A any time since 2001.)

The company's founder, S. Truett Cathy, and subsequent family member leaders have taken a biblically driven approach to doing business, elevating corporate values to be their top priority. They want to make sure that their faith comes through in every decision they make. Check out the corporate purpose:

> "To glorify God by being a faithful steward of all that is entrusted to us. To have a positive influence on all who come in contact with Chick-fil-A."

Take note: There's no mention of those tasty sandwiches or the waffle fries. At Chick-fil-A, honoring God and caring for people (inside and outside the company) are the actions that will translate into product quality and market success. Values first.

As listed on the website, the company's core values include the following:

We're here to serve. We keep the needs of Operators, their Team Members and customers at the heart of our work, doing what is best for the business and best for them.

We're better together. It's through teamwork and collaboration that we do our best work. We're an inclusive culture that leverages the strengths of our diverse talent to innovate and maximize our care for Operators, their Team Members and customers.

We are purpose-driven. We model our Purpose every day, connecting our work and daily activities to our business strategy, supporting each other's efforts to be good stewards who create positive impact on all who come in contact with Chick-fil-A.

We pursue what's next. We find energy in adapting and re-inventing how we do things, from the way we work to how we care for others.

By following those values, the founder of Chick-fil-A decided that his restaurants would be closed on Sundays to allow employees time for church and family. Others in the fast-food industry thought that move was absolutely insane. But Cathy looked to his values in making that decision. How could he honor God and care for people while forcing employees to work on Sundays? He stuck to his guns.

Today, Chick-fil-A is the third largest fast-food restaurant in the country by revenue (behind McDonald's and Starbucks), despite having fewer locations than rivals Taco Bell, Wendy's and Burger King. If you've ever seen the almost-constant lines at their drive-through windows, you know that revenue is coming from hordes of repeat customers.

The lesson here? Values are powerful. They send a loud message to employees and customers alike about what they can expect and what you will deliver.

APPLYING THE STRATEGY

If a commitment to core values helps companies become uncertainty-proof, that begs the question: How can YOU get clear on your core values and use that to produce positive results?

Here are **three steps** that current and future leaders can use to help implement this strategy.

1. Understand your core values.

Managers who work in large, established organizations sometimes feel like this step is unnecessary and want to jump ahead to #2. Not so fast...

Being able to find the page in the employee handbook that lists the core values is not the same as genuinely understanding them. You might be surprised at the insights you can gain by investing the time to dig a little deeper on this subject. Many of my clients can attest to that.

Maybe you are part of a relatively new company and you've never gone through the official process of identifying core values. It might have been an afterthought. Someone had to fill in the blanks on the business plan template before the potential investors showed up for the meeting. Yes, that happens more often than you might think.

Whatever your situation, you can be better prepared to handle uncertainty if you develop a close, personal relationship with your company's core values. This exercise can be an excellent starting point.

EXERCISE: VALUE FINDER

Think about what your company stands for. If your customers were to describe your company, what words would they use? Better yet, what words would you ideally

WANT them to use? Select ALL the choices that apply from the list below or add some of your own.

Accountable	Adaptable	Admirable
Balanced	Big thinking	Bold
Collaborative	Community focused	Constantly improving
Continuously learning	Courageous	Creative
Curious	Customer focused	Disruptive
Diverse	Driven	Empathetic
Employee focused	Environmentally active	Excellence driven
Fast moving	Fearless	Flexible
Fun	Game changing	Hardworking
Helpful	Honest	Hospitable
Humble	Hungry	Impactful
Industry leader	Innovative	Integrity centered
Joyful	Open-minded	Optimistic
Partnership developing	Passionate	Persistent
Pioneering	Positive	Precise
Quality focused	Relationship centered	Relentless
Respectful	Results driven	Service oriented
Strong	Supportive	Sustainability focused
Teamwork centered	Transparent	Trusted
Value producing	Other_____	

While most companies associate with a wide range of attributes, the *core values* are the ones that most resonate and matter for your business. Now for the tough part: Narrow your list down to **FIVE** choices.

If you are doing this exercise as a team, encourage open discussions about which of those words or phrases act as the North Star for your company. Once you come to an agreement, walk away from the list for at least 24 hours. Then revisit the words or phrases to determine whether they feel authentic and inspirational.

Did you nail it? Or does something seem a little off? Keep pushing and exploring until you land on the choices that truly resonate.

For those who went through this process for the first time, congratulations! You've identified your company's core values. If you started this exercise already knowing your organization's stated values, how did your results match up?

2. Use your core values to guide every decision you make.

Some team members automatically assume that applying the core values is a task reserved for the big decisions. Mergers. Acquisitions. The selection of the next CEO. But nothing could be further from the truth!

If you want to protect a business during uncertain times, core values need to be an every-day-all-the-time presence applied across decisions and initiatives of all sizes. For instance:

- Entering new markets
- Communicating with customers
- Expanding to serve a new niche
- Resolving product/service issues
- Extending/adding product lines
- Choosing new vendors
- Establishing strategic partnerships
- Hiring new employees
- Training and developing employees
- Promoting employees
- Engaging and rewarding employees
- Developing policies and procedures
- Interacting with the community/environment

Get in the habit of using your core values as a filter for every choice. Ask yourself these questions: Does this decision align with our core values? Does this person convey those values? Will this technology further our core values or undermine them?

3. Live your core values.

Incorporating core values into decision-making is vital, but some companies have found a way to take that to the next level. They've created cultures in which the core values are woven so tightly into the fabric of the business that they are basically indistinguishable. The employees live and breathe those values. Customers can easily identify the organization's rules of engagement. The brand is fully aligned from the inside out.

One company that falls into that category is Southwest Airlines.

For years, the organization has followed a strategy of reflecting core values from every possible angle. Their process? They hire and train employees who embody their targeted principles for doing business. It's part of their HR DNA. And by creating teams of people who are dedicated to living those values, the employees bring the soul of the company to life for each and every customer.

Core Values for Southwest Airlines

Warrior Spirit	Strive to be the best. Display a sense of urgency. Never give up.
Servant's Heart	Follow the Golden Rule. Treat others with respect. Embrace our Southwest family.
Fun-LUVing Attitude	Be a passionate team player. Don't take yourself too seriously. Celebrate successes.
Wow Our Customers	Deliver world-class hospitality. Create memorable connections. Be famous for friendly service.

Another example comes from Airbnb, the online vacation rental marketplace. The company develops partnerships with homeowners around the world who provide flexible lodging and travel experiences for their end customers.

When the global pandemic arrived in 2020, the travel industry was heavily impacted. Airbnb's business took a direct hit from the unprecedented level of uncertainty that descended like a ferocious storm, and its partners also felt the pain. Since the company had always been deeply connected to its core values, that's the first place leaders turned when they weren't sure what to do next.

First, let's look at the values that drove their response.

Core Values for Airbnb

Champion the Mission	Prioritize work that forwards the company's mission and long-term success while actively participating in the community and culture.
Be a Host	Care for others and make them feel like they belong.
Be a Serial Entrepreneur	Imagine the ideal outcome, be resourceful and bold, and apply original thinking.
Embrace the Adventure	Be curious, demonstrate the potential for growth, ask for help when needed, and bring joy and optimism to your work.

Based on those values, the leaders at Airbnb knew they needed to embrace the adventure rather than waiting patiently for the pandemic to pass. They started to search for long-term solutions rather than short-term fixes. Then they asked themselves, what would a good host do in the middle of a pandemic? The answers seemed obvious.

More than any of their competitors, Airbnb invested time and money to help their homeowner partners clean and sanitize their properties. They used bold thinking to develop a range of innovative solutions, and they pro-vided support by subsidizing additional cleaning costs. They even increased their advertising and promotion, sharing with end customers the efforts being made to create safe travel experiences for them, their families and friends.

Airbnb was able to take swift action in the face of uncertainty by using its core values as a guiding light in a very dark storm.

SEEING THE BIG PICTURE

When you have complete clarity about the values that drive your company, you can minimize the anxiety of decision-making during uncertain times. You'll avoid mis-steps. You'll have the insights to prevent strategic errors. And you may even find a way to leverage those values (despite the odds) for a lasting business advantage.

Make the commitment to use your core values as the grounding force for your organization, and don't let uncertainty allow you to stray from the path.

CHAPTER SIX

Secure Your
BASE

PROCTER & GAMBLE FOUNDED 1837

The world's largest consumer goods company started in 1837 at a kitchen table in Cincinnati, Ohio. Two men who had married sisters were chatting with their father-in-law about their friendly competition for...*wait for it*...animal fat.

Yes, I'm serious.

One of the men, William Procter, was a candlemaker from England. The other, James Gamble, was a soap maker from Ireland. Both of them needed animal fat to create their products. That's when their father-in-law suggested they stop competing for this prime ingredient and go into business together. While they might have initially laughed at that idea, they also saw the brilliance behind it. And shortly after that, the Procter & Gamble Company (P&G) was born.

From the beginning, the founders shared a philosophy about doing business. They recognized that the key to selling more of their products was to understand exactly what their customers wanted and needed. Pretty impressive marketing insights for the 1800s, don't you think? These guys were analyzing the customer experience long before the invention of market research, consumer data mining and social media.

William Procter and James Gamble made it their mission to be in a continuous dialogue with the people who bought their products. Does this meet your needs? How could it be better? What's missing? What other problems around your house are you trying to solve? In many ways, their success can be traced back to the unique, ongoing connections they created with the people responsible for generating their revenue.

One of my favorite examples comes from 1974. A savvy leader at P&G gathered the executive team for an important discussion. His recommendation? To offer a toll-free phone number that customers could call and personally provide product feedback.

I'm guessing that suggestion was initially met with a touch of skepticism.

"Let me get this straight... You want the company to pick up the tab for customers to call us and complain?"

What may have sounded crazy at first was actually a stroke of genius. P&G made it easy (and free!) for customers to provide thoughts, ideas and, yes, even complaints about their products. With that information, the company could quickly make improvements and also develop new products that were, by design, perfectly aligned with shifting customer needs and preferences. P&G repeatedly combined that "intel" with masterful innovation to establish themselves as a dominant market leader.

Want a few examples of how P&G secured their base for greater success over the years?

Customers in the 1870s reported being frustrated by not being able to find their bars of soap when they dropped them in the bathtub.

P&G introduced its first branded product, Ivory Soap, in 1879. It was injected with air so it would float.

....

Customers during the Great Depression shared their concerns about stretching their dollars to feed their families.

P&G introduced a less expensive line of cleaning products, including Dreft Detergent, in 1933.

....

Customers in the 1940s were increasingly concerned about dental health, since dental disease had emerged as one of the most prevalent health issues in the country.

P&G teamed up with scientists to create Crest, the first toothpaste with fluoride that was proven to reduce tooth decay by nearly 50%.

....

Customers in the 1970s were excited about the popularity of electric dryers to help with laundry, but they were frustrated by the annoying static cling.

P&G introduced Bounce dryer sheets in 1975 as an alternative to adding a liquid fabric softener.

....

Customers in the 1990s were leading busy lives and longed for a faster, easier way to clean their homes without all the brooms, mops and buckets.

P&G invented the Swiffer WetJet in 1999 and pioneered an entire product line they call the Quick Clean category.

Today, P&G is one of the largest multinational corporations in America with an extensive global research and development team. From Charmin, Crest and Gillette to Pampers, Olay and Tide, P&G is known for having one of the strongest portfolios of trusted brands in the world. Their success is directly linked to customer relationships and ongoing feedback.

ANALYZING THE APPROACH

When uncertainty hits, many professionals kick into business development overdrive. They worry about attrition and frantically search for new opportunities, new clients, new markets, and new ways to bolster their cash flow. Unfortunately, that approach may be counterproductive.

As P&G demonstrated, your current customers are your best possible resources in the midst of difficult situations. They already know you and like you. They trust you. Strengthening those relationships should be your go-to move when adversity sets in. Reach out to them and start a conversation. Ask how they are being impacted by the uncertainty. Find a meaningful way to help them and solve their problems. That will give you the direction you need to survive and thrive.

Strategy #5
Secure your base during uncertain times. Ongoing dialogue with your current customers will provide the best return on your investment and show you the path forward.

STAYING RELEVANT

One of the biggest mistakes I see professionals make in an uncertain marketplace is continuing to do everything the same way they did pre-uncertainty. Selling the same products. Using the same distribution methods. Marketing the same way. Why?

When customers face the new challenges of uncertain times, their needs change. They still have to buy products, but their purchasing criteria will be different. They'll only buy products they really need, and they'll choose the ones that solve their current and most pressing problems. If companies ignore that shift, their products become irrelevant.

That's why this strategy is so powerful. Securing your base in an uncertain marketplace gives you access to the information you need to remain relevant.

REAPING THE MUTUAL BENEFITS

Companies that fortify their customer relationships during times of uncertainty gain a number of advantages. First, they can collect priceless feedback. As you saw with P&G, many of their iconic brands are proof of that strategy in action.

When you have a direct line of communication with your customers, you can ask them pivotal questions. How should our products and services change to meet your needs *right now*? What are you worried about? What problems are you trying to solve, given the current state of the world? Would your life be better if our products were...faster, cheaper, bigger, smaller, easier to use, longer lasting, more advanced, more flexible, more convenient to purchase?

Think about that for a minute. It's almost like getting the answers to the test before you take it.

If you can find consensus among your customers about an unmet need, you will know exactly what your company needs to do to keep their business and "delight" them along the way. Organizations that are scrambling to find new business during uncertain times miss out on this wealth of information that's ripe for the picking.

Now let's look at securing your base from another angle. At first glance, some people might think grilling customers for market research data during a crisis seems a bit self-serving. In fact, when the right approach is applied, customers don't see it that way at all.

What does it feel like from their perspective?

"This organization recognizes that times are tough for me personally, and they care enough to reach out. They value my opinion and actually take the time to listen to my concerns. If they can use my input to come up with even better products, you can bet I'll be first in line to buy them. What a great company!"

Creating dynamic, two-way conversations with your customers is a smart way to do business, no matter what's happening with the economy, the industry or the world.

But when uncertainty rears its ugly head, it's a must-have for survival. Customers remember who showed up in a crisis. Who reached out, who checked in, and who cared enough to listen.

Short-term and long-term, the mutual benefits of securing your base are striking.

HIGHLIGHTING A MODERN EXAMPLE

Western Water Works (Western) is a Southern California-based business that provides waterworks products to underground contractors and water utilities in California, Oregon, Washington and Utah. The waterworks supply market is highly competitive and dominated by a few large players. Trying to gain market share in this industry is an uphill battle, and pricing pressures can be intense.

The leaders at Western knew they needed to come up with a unique selling proposition or the company would struggle to compete. In the face of economic uncertainty, they decided to focus their energy on their existing clients and secure them before searching for new prospects.

Western began engaging its clients in deeper conversations about their brands, their ultimate goals and the problems they were trying to solve to ensure that their own operations would become more successful. These weren't one-time conversations, mind you. Western's leaders created an ongoing dialogue that allowed them to gain incredible insights into their clients' businesses.

What did Western find out through those conversations? Their clients' biggest frustration was suppliers that didn't hold up their part of the bargain. In fact, company leaders discovered three primary pain points that seemed to resonate with all of the clients they talked to:

1. Inaccurate orders (shipping errors and products that don't meet specifications)
2. Late orders that don't meet the deadlines
3. Inaccurate billing that doesn't match the original quote

No one else in the marketplace was addressing those problems in a defined way. That's when Western's leaders discovered an opportunity to differentiate and position themselves as heroes in their clients' eyes.

They created something new—what they called the Grand Guarantee Club®. Through this program, designed exclusively for its premier clients, Western made a bold promise.

"If you choose us as your supplier, we will ensure a Smooth Running Job® with accurate orders, timely delivery, and accurate billing. Guaranteed! Or we'll give you a $2,000 credit."

Wow. Bold? I'd say that's bold *and* underlined with a red, 72-point font!

Western was willing to go out on a limb to deliver exactly what its clients wanted in a way no other competitor was doing. The response was phenomenal. In an overcrowded marketplace, the company found a creative way to compete and grow. And that was because the leaders listened to their clients and changed their practices to deliver on their promise.

APPLYING THE STRATEGY

Here are **three steps** to help you incorporate this strategy for securing your base, along with an exercise that will guide you through the implementation.

1. Develop a deep relationship with your customers.

Ideally, you've laid the groundwork for this long before uncertainty comes knocking at the door. Develop and maintain an open line of communication with your customers. Build and nurture those relationships. Make that a priority.

So what happens if you find yourself in the middle of a crisis and realize you haven't exactly been diligent about securing your base? Better late than never! Start now and reach out. It matters.

If external forces have you concerned about the future of your business, your customers are probably worried and anxious too. Sometimes the best thing you can do during adversity is to simply show your customers that you're there for them. They will remember that.

In Chapter One, I shared with you the story about the devastating floods that wiped out my husband's dental practice. We spent weeks in the mud, combing through any remnants from the office that might be salvageable. The process was physically and emotionally draining, and we felt like it would never end.

Every day for three weeks, right at noon, a local insurance agent arrived in his pickup truck. He stood in the truck bed and handed out free sandwiches and water to all of us who were doing the back-breaking work to recover our businesses. In many ways, his big smile and words of encouragement were just as nourishing as the lunch he provided. We will never forget his kindness.

Approximately half of the businesses in the impacted office complex already used this man for their insurance needs, although we did not. Once we rebuilt and were ready to insure the new property, guess who we called? Wasn't even a question. This man was there when times were tough, and that's the kind of person we wanted to do business with.

When uncertainty is affecting everyone, just showing up and proving that you are there for your customers will have a lasting impact.

2. Listen, listen, listen.

Ongoing dialogue is a critical part of securing your base. Sounds simple, right? No so much. Company representatives often want to dominate the customer conversations, trying to cram in as many feature/benefit messages as possible. Sell, sell, sell. That's not a helpful approach in general. But when uncertainty has turned the world upside down, it's a killer.

Instead, ask questions—and listen like your success depends on it. (It does!)

Uncertainty has a way of changing the preferences of your customers. If you don't listen carefully, you'll miss out on the clues that can define those changes. What are they saying that they want and need now? What's the subtext of their messages? What other details can you pull out of their comments?

Your customers will essentially tell you exactly what they want to buy, how and where they want to buy it, and how much they're willing to spend. Your future action plan is right there in their comments. You simply have to listen to find it.

Depending on the size of your company and the quantity of your customers, listening opportunities may take on different forms. Commercial or industrial businesses might have regular phone calls or meetings, one-on-one, with their clients. Retail companies could use surveys, focus groups, website comments and social media chatter to take the pulse of their buyers.

Another form of listening? Detailed feedback from customer service teams and frontline salespeople. If those representatives ask thoughtful questions and listen intently, they can unearth valuable information about product wish lists and hidden roadblocks that haven't yet come to light. Make sure your company or employer has procedures in place to gather that kind of information and funnel it to departments that have the ability to use it. Which brings us to the last step...

3. Apply the knowledge.

In and of itself, listening doesn't really do any good. Current and future leaders have to get creative and find ways to apply what they've learned about the shifting needs of their existing customers.

P&G taught a master class on how to do this. I doubt they had an official R&D department in the 1800s, but I'll bet infusing soap with air never crossed their minds. However, their customers expressed a problem. They listened. And they created a meaningful solution. By closing that feedback loop, customers were happy and sales went through the roof. Everybody won.

EXERCISE: STAYING RELEVANT

If you find yourself in the middle of a crisis or a major episode of uncertainty, you can reground yourself by having conversations with your current customers. The following exercise will guide you in securing your base and staying relevant.

a. **Make a list of everyone you have done business with in the last two years**. Include any customers who are not currently active. This will be your starting point for the exercise. Eventually you can expand your efforts to include all previous customers and even the potential ones that did not end in sales.

b. **Set a schedule to call each one of them**. Try reaching out to two or three customers per day, as your calendar allows. Make it a priority.

c. **Focus on relationship-building.** The purpose of your calls is simply to check in and see how they are doing. No efforts to sell or upgrade. Just ask questions that communicate how much you value the relationship.

- How are things going with you? How about your business?
- How are the current challenges impacting your company and industry?
- How are the current challenges impacting your customers?
- What are you focused on right now? What is your top priority?

Trust me, these will be the easiest calls you ever make. Customers want to hear from you. They will appreciate your interest and concern. And they will remember your kindness.

   d. **Actively listen.** Take notes. Write everything down. In between the small talk, you will hear about their opportunities and concerns. What's working? What's not working? What pesky problems are keeping them awake at night?

   e. **Identify the common threads.** After you've completed the first 25 calls, review your notes and look for any themes or commonalities that emerge. What are the similarities or trends? Keep testing to find the shared experiences that deserve attention.

   f. **Find ways to apply what you learned.** The information you gain on these calls is the gift that helps you understand how your products and services need to shift to remain relevant in the marketplace. The more you can apply that information, the more attractive and competitive your products and services will be to your customers and prospects.

     ◆ Increase the value of your products with tweaks and add-ons that better meet changing needs.

     ◆ Develop new products and services that solve current problems.

- ◆ Brainstorm to find innovative approaches or strategic partnerships that meet needs in a fresh way.

- ◆ Change the messaging used to position your products so that it resonates more directly with customers' shifting preferences.

- ◆ Integrate existing customers' language to attract new businesses that are likely looking to solve the same types of problems.

By completing (and later expanding) this exercise, you will be well on your way to securing your base, creating more loyal customers, increasing new-business referrals, and strengthening your market position as a relevant, agile company.

SEEING THE BIG PICTURE

Ongoing relationships with your customers form the foundation of your continued success. That applies whether the stock market is at an all-time high or hitting rock bottom. But in times of uncertainty, leveraging those relationships will provide you with the best possible return on investment.

Remember it's a myth that customers don't spend money during economic challenges. They do! But they are purchasing products and services that are relevant for that exact moment in time. Securing your base ensures that you can meet their fluctuating needs in a targeted way.

Current and future leaders who intentionally reach out to their customers in tough times gain the opportunity to communicate empathy and compassion, further cementing those connections. They can gather information that leads them forward in a very targeted way. And they can build a level of loyalty that's destined to withstand price-slashing competitors, natural disasters, and stock market meltdowns.

When everything around you is swirling in chaos, securing your base is the insurance policy you need to remain relevant.

CHAPTER SEVEN

Build Your
NETWORK

CRANE & COMPANY FOUNDED 1801

Question: What do these things have in common? Exquisite corporate letterhead. A $10 bill. And late-night comedian Jimmy Fallon's famous Thank You Notes.

Answer: They are all printed on paper from Crane & Co.

Let's start at the beginning to find out how that happened.

In 1770, an entrepreneur named Stephen Crane purchased the Liberty Paper Mill outside of Boston, Massachusetts, and began to develop a market for his paper. One of his earliest customers? Oddly enough, it was Paul Revere, a patriot in the American Revolution. Revere used Crane's products to print the first paper money for the American colonies. *(Foreshadowing alert!)*

Stephen's son, Zenas Crane, ventured out in 1779 to open a new mill in Dalton, Massachusetts, and he officially founded Crane & Co. in 1801. To produce his paper, he needed local housewives to provide him with their old rags, which he would beat to a pulp and use as the raw material. The problem? Without a steady supply of rags, his business came to a screeching halt.

Crane invested time and money to build relationships with these "suppliers," and he even started advertising to find new sources. He knew that developing connections with his rag vendors was just as important as developing connections with his customers. Crane made it his mission to build personal relationships with *all* of the people responsible for his business success.

In 1865, the paper mill burned to the ground. How's that for a big serving of uncertainty? While rebuilding was under way, Zenas Marshall Crane (Stephen's grandson) spent some time in Europe learning how to create high-quality stationery that was becoming all the rage in the US. When he went back home and incorporated those techniques, Crane & Co. enjoyed a big bump in business.

Some of the nation's most elite companies like Marshall Field's, Tiffany & Co. and Bailey Banks & Biddle became loyal customers. And when it was time to create invitations for the ceremony to dedicate the Statue of Liberty, Crane & Co. paper was the natural choice.

By 1873, W. Murray Crane (Stephen's great-grandson) joined the company and used his significant networking skills to attract a wide range of new customers. His most notable success? He secured a contract with the US

Treasury to provide paper for America's currency. Those government connections continued to pay off, as Murray Crane went on to serve as both the governor and senator in Massachusetts from 1904 to 1913.

Things looked bleak for many paper mills during the Great Depression, but Crane & Co. scrambled to stay in business by operating 24/7 to produce the paper for war bonds. The company's hard work was also rewarded after World War II with a number of lucrative projects. Wall Street bought Crane's paper for stock certificates. Architects started using it for their blueprints. Even Queen Elizabeth II insisted on Crane paper for the messages in her despatch boxes.

By the 1980s, more uncertainty loomed on the horizon. Foreign competitors were threatening to steal away big chunks of Crane's business with the Treasury Department. That's when a long-time friend and associate of the Crane family, US Representative Silvio Conte, stepped in to propose a law to protect them. Passed in 1987, this legislation prevents foreign-owned companies from supplying paper for US currency. It's safe to say, that relationship added significant value.

Today, Crane & Co. is a global organization that produces and sells top-quality stationery, paper systems for business, wedding invitations and greeting cards. And, of course, it has been the sole supplier of currency paper for the US Treasury since 1879.

Relationships were, hands down, the heart and soul of the business. Crane & Co. used its considerable network to build more meaningful connections, find new opportunities in challenging times and turn uncertainty into competitive advantage.

ANALYZING THE APPROACH

Our lives and our businesses are defined by our connections. Think about what that looks like in real life. Maybe a friend introduced you to your significant other. A neighbor mentioned a potential business lead that turned out to be your biggest client. The stranger you started chatting with at the airport ended up being your best employee.

The size of your network and the quality of your connections determine the trajectory of your success. Relationships translate into opportunities.

The Crane family implicitly understood this concept. They were master networkers. Now, for some people, the word "networking" conjures up images of a crowded room with people hurriedly exchanging business cards near a stale cheese platter. What we're talking about here is so much deeper. And wider. And broader.

Crane & Co. built a monumental business because of its relationships with vendors, local citizens, customers, government contacts and more. Those connections sustained the organization during times of great uncertainty and directly contributed to its long-term success. That same strategy can be a game-changer for you, as well.

Strategy #6
Build your network in a strategic way, and be deliberate about making connections. Invest in those relationships with consistent contact and proactive support.

DEFINING THE TRUE IMPACT

Prepare yourself for a big, bold, bulletproof statement: _If you build your network, it will change your life._ If you think that sounds melodramatic, give me a chance to prove you wrong. Keep reading!

One of the very first things I do every day is network. Now, I have a cup of coffee first, read my relentless vision and then I decide who I am going to network with.

Connecting with no agenda, no self-interest; just reaching out to invest in another person—that is networking.

A few years ago, I reached out to connect with one of my favorite contacts, Trish Springfield. Trish and I met when I was doing some consulting work with her company.

Every so often, I would reach out and give her a call, comment on social media, or send her a short email. Always just investing in Trish, her job and her life. On one of those random calls, Trish was having some big challenges in her business, and we ended up talking for over an hour.

At the end of the call, she caught herself almost embarrassed that she had not asked much about me. I assured her that was fine and just closed by telling her I was going to send her a copy of my new book.

About a month later, Trish called me to let me know she loved the book so much that she had shared it with her boss, the CEO of the company. He wanted to know if I would be interested in coming down to talk with their leadership team.

BOOM! I had gotten a job simply from networking, simply from investing in others. I flew down and spoke for their leadership team, and that went so well the CEO hired me to speak for their entire team at their annual meeting. BOOM! I had now gotten two jobs simply from networking and investing in others.

After speaking for their entire team, the CEO hired me to redesign and fully implement their sales training.

BOOM! Simply from networking, investing in others, I landed the biggest contract to date in my career.

A fantastic testament to the power of networking, even if the story ended here—but it doesn't!

One year after completing that contract, Trish referred me to a friend of hers who ran a company in Honolulu, Hawaii. They hired me first to speak for their leadership team, then to speak at their annual meeting and then ultimately to redesign and implement their sales training—a contract worth twice as much as the one with Trish's company that came with a monthly trip to Honolulu first class.

Build your network. It will change your business and your life.

BUILDING UP SOCIAL CAPITAL

In many ways, having a relationship with a network partner is like a bank account. People make "deposits" to build relationships over time in the form of contacts, referrals, sales, support and information. Then, when adversity hits, they have the credibility to make a "withdrawal"—a request for the same type of aid they were willing to provide. It's a mutually beneficial system of social capital.

But those kinds of relationships don't form overnight. Building solid connections takes time. Far too often, people wait to network until they need something. The crisis has already occurred. The challenge is underway.

The moral of that story? Don't wait. Start networking now!

Make a commitment to identify people with the potential to be outstanding network partners. *(More on that subject toward the end of this chapter.)* Meet them or reintroduce yourself, get to know them, and take a genuine interest in learning about them. Ask great, open-ended questions, and listen carefully to their responses.

What do they do and what are their business goals? What are their unique skills and experiences? What information do they have access to? What people are they connected with?

The more you know about your network partners, the better equipped you are to proactively offer your support.

Here's my best piece of advice on this subject: Invest in others before you ask them to invest in you. Returning to my previous example, it's harder to make a withdrawal if you haven't been making regular deposits.

Be intentional about helping the people in your network, even before they make a request. How could you add value for them? Do you have information, resources or referrals that might help them reach their goals? Stay in touch regularly and provide support whenever you can.

From that standpoint, think about networking as a lifestyle rather than a task. It's not a single event. It's something professionals should do every day as part of their normal operating procedures. The results that emerge from that type of long-term, continuous, proactive networking can be incredible. And when major waves of uncertainty leave you gasping for air, you'll have some dedicated partners who are willing to throw you a much-needed lifeline.

HIGHLIGHTING A MODERN EXAMPLE

A young woman named Sharon Pryse started working as a bank clerk, with no discernable direction on how to move beyond that role. But when she volunteered to help her boss with an unusual project, she changed the trajectory of her career.

Sharon's boss was unable to drive but really wanted to go to church every morning before work. Sharon stepped up and offered to take her. Now, at this point in her life, Sharon was not a churchgoer. But after visiting the church with her boss on a daily basis, she really felt at home there. Even when she wasn't driving her boss, she felt drawn to the church. She started attending services, participating in Sunday School, and volunteering to help at special events. She had become a "regular."

That's when Father Dan, who was the minister at that time, asked her to join a committee to talk about raising money for the expansion of the church. Sharon had no idea what that would entail, but she enthusiastically agreed.

When she arrived for the first meeting, she found herself in a room with some of the most powerful and influential leaders in the community and the state. This group of people represented a wealth of knowledge, skills, contacts and power. If she hadn't been willing to drive someone to church and join a committee, she would never have made these priceless connections.

Over the next few years, Sharon built relationships with these movers and shakers. She invested in her network and her community. Every time she offered her time and her help, she made another connection. She found another opportunity. Another open door.

Today, Sharon is the founder and CEO of The Trust Company, arguably one of the most prestigious financial services firms in the Southeast. Sharon will be the first to tell you the success she achieved both personally and professionally stems from connections she has made through the years. She invested in people and in her community, and her investment was returned tenfold.

APPLYING THE STRATEGY

To incorporate this strategy, you'll want to take intentional steps toward creating and strengthening three different types of business networks: an internal network, an external network, and a resource network. The following exercise will give you a head start.

1. Build your internal network.

Begin by making a list of the top ten people within your company or industry who would be considered valuable connections. Which relationships are essential to help you do your job more effectively?

These people might include the CEO of your company, the VP of operations, the IT director, a department manager, a remarkably creative co-worker, the president of your industry organization, or even a trusted colleague at your primary competitor.

To help you create your list, consider some qualifying questions:

- Which people within your company/industry *directly* impact your ability to be successful?
- Which people within your company/industry *indirectly* impact your ability to be successful?
- Who within your company/industry is highly respected, influential and well-connected?
- Who do you admire for an outstanding work ethic and impressive achievements?
- Who has previously been successful in your current role, as well as the one you aspire to?

In many cases, you may already have relationships with some of these people. The point here is to make the connections more strategic and intentional. By taking a proactive approach to building and maintaining your internal network, you can establish a baseline of essential support throughout the most critical areas of your company and industry.

2. Expand your external business network.

The next step is to think beyond the immediate bubble of your organization. Make a list of your top 10 clients, your top 10 referral sources, and top 10 community leaders. Community leaders might include an executive with your chamber of commerce, a board member with a local business club, or a government official.

These qualifying questions may be helpful in guiding you to think about the relationships that add value to your business or your professional role:

- Which clients generate the most revenue for your company?
- Have you developed relationships with these clients that go beyond transactions?
- How did you originally get the leads for those clients?
- What other referral sources have resulted in prosperous clients/projects?
- *(Existing clients, strategic partners, vendors, neighbors, friends/family, etc.)*
- Has community involvement or visibility produced tangible business advantages for you? *(New*

customers, unexpected information sources, preferential treatment, etc.)

- What people within the community would be valuable partners to help develop or expand those advantages?

Make it a point to stay firmly connected with these people who have the power to impact your success. Check in regularly and stay in touch, offering to help whenever you can. Even unsolicited. This style of targeted networking is one of the most effective ways to build your professional reputation, and it will undoubtedly produce a strong return on investment.

3. Increase your resources.

No matter how smart and talented we are, we can't be the best at everything. It's just not possible. But thankfully, we don't have to be. We just need to know other people who are ready and willing to fill in the gaps. If we fortify those relationships, we can create an unstoppable synergy that withstands adversity.

Think of it this way. If you had the misfortune to be stranded on a deserted island with two other people, your outlook is better if each person brings some unique skills to the table. Your odds for survival go up if one person knows how to fish, one knows how to build a sturdy shelter, and the other is an expert on plants. Together, you'll last much longer than, say, three carpenters. And you won't starve to death. That's the concept.

If you can surround yourself with people who have contrasting skills and talents, you'll have a resource network that can tangibly expand your success. Maybe you need access to someone who is an innovative thinker, a visionary strategic planner, a technology guru, a great project manager, or someone who is politically connected. Take the time to find the right people.

These questions can help you identify the best people for your resource network:

- What skills (beyond your own) are required for you to become more successful?
- Who do you know that has those skills and applies them at a high level?
- If you were going to hire three consultants to support your efforts, who would you choose?
- Who would you want in your corner if you were facing a significant challenge?
- What skills do they have? Do you know others with similar skills?

Sometimes it's easier to reach out to people who have more in common with us. Don't give in to that tendency. Stretch to make connections with people who can bring a diversity of thoughts and skills to your resource network.

That will amplify your potential, no matter what direction the NASDAQ is heading.

SEEING THE BIG PICTURE

Building and maintaining a powerful network takes time and commitment. But that network needs to be in place long before you face the challenges of uncertainty.

Be strategic about selecting the connections inside and outside of your company with the most potential to accelerate your success. Get to know them and understand their challenges. Invest in them first and do what you can to add value. Keep in touch regularly. And when the storms come, your connections will be there to sustain you until the dark clouds have passed.

CHAPTER EIGHT

Strengthen
YOUR TEAM

ATKINS & PEARCE FOUNDED 1817

You might not be familiar with Atkins & Pearce, but I'm betting you have some products around your home that were made by this high-performance textile manufacturer.

Got any decorative candles in your dining room? The wicks were likely crafted by Atkins & Pearce. How about a fishing pole? Yep, the fishing line may have originated from the same company. Ditto for the strings that connect any of the blinds on your windows. And if you happen to have any electrical or digital devices (and who doesn't these days?), Atkins & Pearce probably made the casings and sleeves for those plugs or charger cords.

When a worldwide product requires a high-tech fiber solution, Atkins & Pearce usually gets the call. Here's how it all started.

Shortly after the American Revolution, two brothers named John and Henry Pearce arrived in Cleveland, Ohio, and they were fascinated by the way Eli Whitney's invention of the cotton gin had transformed the economy. That sparked their entrepreneurial spirit.

What if this already-brilliant machine could do more than just separate the cotton fibers from the seeds and actually spin the cotton into fabric? A few strategic modifications later, the brothers produced an updated version of the cotton gin—and a new business was formed in 1817. They discovered growing demand when they started selling this advanced equipment to cotton processors and plantations.

As tensions mounted in the 1850s with the threat of Civil War, the brothers began contemplating an adjustment to their business model. The company ultimately shifted from selling its machines to the processing cotton and textiles in-house, which is an approach it continues to use today.

Originally known as Gould Pearce & Co., the business changed its name to Atkins & Pearce after one of the Pearce sisters married a man named H.T. Atkins in 1880. He quickly assumed a leadership role with the organization, as did their children over the years.

During the Great Depression and World War II, a fifth-generation family member, Asa Atkins, was at the helm of the company. He recognized the potential for a steep downturn in business and made a strategic pivot.

The organization survived the lean times by manufacturing parachute cords and other supplies for the military.

Once the financial markets recovered, Atkins & Pearce returned to its roots and focused on developing advanced candlewicks and commercial/industrial textiles. The company moved its headquarters to Covington, Kentucky, in 1986 and expanded into a 550,000-square-foot manufacturing facility in 2008.

Today, Atkins & Pearce provides customized, fiber-based solutions for a diverse set of customers across the globe. The company is run by the seventh generation of the same family in 2020 and has more than 250 employees.

So how did this family-run business turn into a worldwide phenomenon that survived and thrived during some of our country's toughest moments? The secret lies within those 250 employees.

As you might guess, not all of them are family members. But if you interviewed them, you'd get some version of this same story:

They overwhelmingly *feel* like part of the family.

They are treated like family.

They are trusted like family.

They take pride in their work, just as if they were family members/owners.

That's it! That's the key. A team with this kind of loyalty is essentially unbeatable.

Leaders at Atkins & Pearce always believed the employees were their biggest competitive advantage. They invested in them, and they were relentless about supporting them. Apparently that strategy paid off—and it continues to reap benefits for them today.

Want some proof?

The multi-generational leadership at Atkins & Pearce is also mirrored in the employee population, where working for this company has become a family tradition.

When a newspaper in Ohio did research for an article about the company's impressive history, the reporter interviewed one man who remembered taking a tour of the factory as a young child with his father, a long-time employee of Atkins & Pearce. As an adult, he also worked for the company for more than 30 years, alongside multiple cousins and uncles who had followed the same path. Their story wasn't an anomaly. Dozens of families have made employment with Atkins & Pearce part of their legacy. For them, the company is...just like family.

Is it a coincidence that this powerhouse, employee-honoring company has stayed in business for more than two centuries, despite plenty of uncertainty? I think not!

ANALYZING THE APPROACH

Successful companies—even those that appear to set themselves apart by their innovative technology—know that their teams are the true differentiator. Their market distinction. Their protection during difficult moments in history.

It might be a stretch to think about the Pearce brothers' updated cotton gin as a high-tech innovation, but it really was cutting-edge in 1817. They could easily have gotten swept up in the features and benefits of their fancy invention and considered their employees to be easily replaceable resources. Instead, they realized the indisputable value of their team members to sell their products and, more importantly, to come up with new inventions.

The same holds true today. Even though Atkins & Pearce has a massive facility lined with 13,000 braiding machines, leaders there know that their success is based on the creative minds that come up with customized solutions for their clients. Machines can't do that; people can.

When uncertainty hits, there's very little that leaders can control. But they can choose the people who surround them while they wait for adversity to pass. If those employees are equally passionate about the survival and growth of the business, long-term success is inevitable.

> **Strategy #7**
>
> **Strengthen your team to create an unbreakable barrier against the threats of uncertainty. By investing in great people, you'll create a powerful competitive advantage.**

SIMPLIFYING THE EQUATION

OK, I'll admit it. Developing a strong team might not initially sound like a hidden business secret. Thousands of leadership books and articles have been written about teamwork and employee engagement. But sometimes I wonder if those phrases have slipped into cliché territory. Are we starting to gloss over the real meaning behind them? High attendance at the Q2 Sales Kickoff meeting doesn't automatically equate to high engagement.

If we want teamwork with the capacity to carry our companies through harsh environments, we need to get laser-focused on this issue.

Jack Welch, legendary businessman and the former CEO of GE, once told leaders they needed to concentrate on three things to be successful: Cashflow, Customer Experience, and Employee Engagement.

Welch makes a great point. But I actually believe it's less complicated than that. (Sorry, Jack!)

If your company is overly focused on cashflow, you run the risk of alienating your customers and losing your top employees.

If you try to make all of your customers happy all the time, you'll go bankrupt.

But if you surround yourself with the best and brightest talent, invest in their development, and deliberately create a culture that keeps them engaged and motivated, you'll have everything you need to be successful. Your team will be inspired to create an outstanding customer experience that will naturally drive amazing cashflow.

Atkins & Pearce makes an excellent case for that singular priority of employee engagement. When current and future leaders want to deliver the maximum ROI and ensure their organization's survival in an uncertain marketplace, building a vibrant team is the way to make that happen. Everything else falls into place if they get that part right.

UNDERSTANDING THE MINDSET

When I talk with my clients about intensifying the teamwork within their organizations to sustain them in economic downturns, many of them want to dive head-first into the process pool.

"Let's add more training."

"We need some weekend team-building retreats."

"Monthly lunches and happy hours!"

"How about 'Trust-Fall Fridays'?"

Nope. Hit the brakes on all of that for a moment.

You can't build a meaningful relationship with someone unless you get to know them. *Really know them.* The first thing leaders at all levels need to do is to understand the mindset of each employee. What really matters to them? What motivates them? What does uncertainty feel like in their shoes?

In trying times, team members are likely to be distracted by the valid fears about downsizing, outsourcing, furloughs, mergers or acquisitions. And, the truth is, you can't guarantee that none of those things will happen. But you can replace that guarantee with something else that is even more powerful: a corporate culture where they feel understood, valued, appreciated and respected.

If you've made the effort to create or support that kind of culture within your company, people won't be scrambling for the door during a crisis. They will stand right beside you, fighting and clawing for survival as a cohesive team.

The point here? Get to know the people you work with, and build genuine relationships with them. Take the time to do it right and create authentic, personal connections. As you do that, here's something to keep in mind.

This one comes from the don't-judge-a-book-by-its-cover file. As you develop relationships with the people from your company, department or team, avoid the temptation to stereotype and clump individuals into groups that don't actually represent their unique attributes, thoughts and preferences.

When I was younger, I remember my dad coming home from work and declaring that the world would end if those "crazy twenty-somethings" were in charge. That attitude is fairly standard across the board and across time.

Think of all the sitcoms in recent years that portray Millennials as urban-dwelling, self-centered and digitally addicted. How about Baby Boomers? Oh, they are all materialistic suburbanites who have to call tech support at least twice a week. Since the time of Socrates, older people have complained about younger people—and vice versa.

While every generation grows up in a different environment that can make them seem almost foreign to the others, shift to think about that as a genuine advantage.

Millennials might have natural instincts about ways to use technology to more effectively communicate with customers and promote products. Boomers may have the experience and wisdom to navigate difficult situations they've been through before. Each generation has value to offer, so it's important to sideline the stereotypes and find the distinctive contributions made by each individual.

Beyond that realization, force yourself to remove the labels. You might just discover a 65-year-old digital genius and a 30-year-old with the maturity to develop innovative strategies.

Don't get hung up on faulty assumptions. Treat each person with respect, and take the time to uncover their one-of-a-kind qualities.

HIGHLIGHTING A MODERN EXAMPLE

Brian Holland and his brother Stan founded a mortgage lending company in Virginia Beach, Virginia, in 1997. Brian served as the CEO for Atlantic Bay Mortgage Company, while Stan was COO.

The mortgage business was already challenging, with numerous competitors, frequent consolidation of companies, and constant regulatory changes. Then online lenders like Quicken Loans and Rocket Mortgage flooded the market. While consumers had the benefit of many different choices, lending companies were struggling to differentiate themselves.

The brothers at Atlantic Bay believed that their people would be their strongest competitive advantage. These employees were the key to delivering the excellent customer service that was reflected in the company's value statement:

We Genuinely Care	Put people first.
Inspire Growth	Adapt and improve with passionate positivity.
Have Fun	Love what we do while making a difference.

Brian and Stan knew that creating a culture that inspired employees was the most direct path to an exceptional customer experience. As leaders, their top two priorities are their people and their revenue, in that order. And they don't intend to outsource those goals to others on their leadership team.

Brian and Stan created an office environment that was professional but also fun. They play engaging games and offer a selection of great snacks. Employees are given the flexibility to work at their own pace and manage their days, as long as they are accountable for their workload and meet their deadlines. The brothers also frequently host breakfast or dinner gatherings for employees, just so they can get to know them better.

The offices are also very family friendly. Both Brian and Stan are open about leaving the office to attend their children's sporting events, and they are quick to encourage their team members to do the same.

Facing the constant challenges of regulation, competition and fluctuating interest rates, the leaders at

Atlantic Bay understand that their business can thrive during uncertainty if they are diligent about investing in their team.

APPLYING THE STRATEGY

Rock-solid companies tend to have cultures that make people feel a passion for the purpose, the pride of ownership, and an unshakable level of loyalty. For current and future leaders, these **three steps** can help you accomplish that goal.

1. Communicate the purpose.

Team members want to do work that matters, and they want to know they are making a difference. When they genuinely feel like they are part of something bigger than themselves, their level of commitment increases exponentially. They desperately want to have a purpose.

I already talked about the importance of getting to know your employees or direct reports as part of the relationship-building process; this is the other side of that coin. Make sure your team members really know your company. Help them recognize its core values. Its brand personality. Its attitude toward everything from tackling business challenges to interacting with people inside and outside of the organization. Help them become part of the purpose.

When people understand the company's purpose and can directly see how their efforts are moving toward that, they become emotionally connected to the goal. They internalize it. They are inspired by it. And they become passionate about supporting it.

EXERCISE: PINPOINTING YOUR PURPOSE

Sometimes the true purpose of a business can get lost in between the deadlines, the deliverables and the daily reports. It's time to move that back to the forefront and make it the centerpiece for everything you do.

Bring together a group of organizational or team leaders to brainstorm and discuss the answers to these questions.

- Why are we in business? *(Hint: think beyond making money!)*
- Why do we do what we do?
- What propels us to do this better than anyone else?
- What's the meaning behind our success?
- How well do we project that meaning, internally and externally?
- How well do we communicate that purpose to our employees?

If you don't already have a prominent purpose statement, use your answers to craft one. Here are a few examples:

Dove	Achieving real beauty and encouraging women to love themselves
Patagonia	Inspiring and implementing sustainability in the outdoor industry
Crayola	Fostering creativity in children
Coca-Cola	Spreading and sharing happiness
Atkins & Pearce	To enhance our customer's ability to achieve their growth strategy faster and with less risk

2. Instill ownership.

Do the people in your company feel like valuable contributors or little cogs in a giant wheel? That perception is determined by the culture. If you've helped to create an environment that invites participation rather than blocks it, you're ahead of the game.

Make sure you are giving team members an opportunity for ownership. (I'm not referring to stock options here, although those are always great, too.)

Before you add layers of HR benefits, consider how workers are treated with respect to decisions, strategies and project approaches. Do they generally feel like they have a voice and a vote? Or are they told what to do and expected to do it without complaints?

Admittedly, getting input from more people takes time and effort. But remember there are several advantages. From the perspective of two-heads-are-better-than-one, you increase your odds of coming up with superior ideas by casting a wider net. Plus, people like to support what they have helped to create and build.

Atkins & Pearce provides us with a great example. Their culture is founded on what they describe as a "we care" policy. They encourage every team member to communicate candidly and respectfully. It's more than just being interested in what employees have to say. Leaders deliberately seek out their opinions, and employees know that their thoughts and ideas really matter.

EXERCISE: OWNERSHIP ASSESSMENT

Start by gathering a group of leaders or managers together to assess your company's capacity to instill ownership in its employees.

- Do you lead through the power of questions?
- Do you ask for (and listen to) the opinions of your team members?
- Do you invite them to submit their ideas?
- Do you provide opportunities for those ideas and opinions to flow freely through the organization?

- Do you have an unspoken bias toward ideas that come from people with the most senior titles?
- What insights might you be missing if you don't listen more intentionally to frontline workers and employees at every level of the company?

If you discover that you haven't been consistent in instilling a sense of ownership among your team members, you can easily develop this new habit by following this process:

- List the three biggest challenges your business is facing right now.
- Distill those challenges into a concise format with key variables defined.
- Ask your team members for their ideas and strategies to solve those problems.
- Incorporate their feedback when developing strategies to move forward.
- Express appreciation to them for their contributions.
- Communicate frequently with them about progress and "wins."

3. Provide value.

So far, so good. You've helped people to understand your organization's purpose and given them opportunities for ownership. Before you can truly expect them to invest in your company long-term, it's your job as leaders to invest in them.

So how can you provide value for your team members?

The obvious answers include a competitive salary, benefits package, rewards and incentives. And those are important components not to be overlooked! But surprisingly, the two things that employees say they want most from their companies are *support* and *accountability*.

Employees want leaders who are open and transparent about their expectations. They feel most comfortable when supervisors set the rules for the game and explain exactly how success will be measured. And then—this is equally important—they want leaders who will enforce the rules.

Team members who follow those rules and meet or exceed expectations should get rewarded. Those who are the proverbial "dead weight" shouldn't be allowed to slide while the dutiful rule-followers pick up the slack. When leaders create an atmosphere of fairness and responsible follow-through, employees have a much higher level of job satisfaction.

Employees also want to know that their individual development matters to the company. Their career goals. Their professional hopes and dreams. When employees are provided with training, development and coaching, they have definitive proof that the organization recognizes their potential and wants to help them fulfill that. Talk about a big-time, loyalty-building investment!

Companies can extend that concept by developing a comprehensive and transparent succession plan. This gives employees valuable input about the trajectory of their careers and provides them with an enormous incentive to stick around rather than jumping to a competitor.

Having a shared vision for the future adds value for employees and organizations alike.

EXERCISE: TARGETED DEVELOPMENT

Assemble a group of key leaders who can put the following value-added program into place. The scope of the exercise may vary depending on your professional role, as well as on the size and structure of your company or employer.

- Select the top 3–5 employees on your team or within each department.
- Communicate your current goals, expectations, and rationale.
- Perform a gap analysis to determine if they need any additional skills or training to achieve those goals.
- Eliminate any unnecessary roadblocks by giving them access to the required resources.
- Coach and support them at least monthly to help them grow and monitor their progress.

- Evaluate any changes in attitudes, commitment levels and performance every six months.
- Expand the program over time based on your results and time constraints.

When you make it a priority to invest in building a dynamic and cohesive team, your organization becomes fueled by the superpowers of fiercely committed internal advocates. There's nothing else quite like it.

Educate your employees about the true purpose of your business. Help them grow and develop. Offer them new opportunities. Keep them engaged. Provide attractive incentives and rewards for their hard work. Give them support and accountability. And by doing all of that consistently, you can create a rare brand of teamwork with a family-bond level of loyalty—one that can't be toppled by the cruel slap of uncertainty. Pretty extraordinary stuff.

SEEING THE BIG PICTURE

Current and future leaders who make it a priority to strengthen their teams are primary contributors to companies that withstand the test of time and the ongoing threats of uncertainty. They know that their people *are* their advantage.

This strategy is about much more than having an attractive benefits package and an espresso machine in the breakroom. Leaders at these companies actually work to build relationships with their employees, and they ensure that every team member understands the company's purpose.

Likewise, these leaders get to the know the purpose behind each employee. They demonstrate their support through development training and career pathway planning, as well as a culture that gives them a sense of ownership and responsibility.

When companies create this kind of environment and leaders develop relationships with employees, every person on the payroll is fully invested in achieving success. That's a team that's tough to beat.

CHAPTER NINE

Shed Fast and
KEEP MOVING

C.F. MARTIN & COMPANY FOUNDED 1833

Christian Frederick Martin grew up in Germany and learned the art of guitar making from his father. To further refine his skills, he took a job working as an apprentice in Vienna with one of Europe's most renowned guitar makers, Johann Stauffer. Martin then moved to New York City in the early 1830s, where the US guitar market was still in its infancy.

He saw great opportunity in the anticipated growth, so he founded C.F. Martin & Co. in 1833.

To help develop a customer base for his acoustic guitars, he focused on distribution through teachers, importers and wholesalers.

Although business was booming, Martin and his family quickly tired of the hustle and bustle in New York, relocating to Nazareth, Pennsylvania, in 1839. Their attitude?

If it's not working, change it! The scenery and pace of life in Nazareth made them feel much more at home, and the business has remained there ever since.

When many instruments were lost or destroyed in the Civil War, Martin produced a variety of different guitars in new styles to help musicians get back to performing. His introduction of the smaller, parlor-sized guitars was particularly well-received, and his dedication to serving these customers was also quite profitable. The business continued to flourish.

Christian Martin passed away in 1873 and left the company to his son and namesake, Christian Martin, Jr. Unfortunately, the younger Martin died unexpectedly in 1888, which put his son Frank Henry in charge.

That sounds like it should have been an easy leadership transition within the family business—except that Frank was only 22 years old at the time. Handing over the reins of a successful business to someone who was barely a legal adult could have been a disaster. But, as it turned out, it was a really good thing. Frank more than exceeded expectations.

Perhaps because of his youth, Frank was very much in tune with the rapidly changing musical tastes of that time and the more relaxed culture that was spreading across the country. He had a clear vision for the organization to stay on the front edge of that trend and capture market share before his competitors could respond.

Frank followed that strategy and shed the old plan for manufacturing. He began producing different types of guitars that better met the shifting needs of his customers. He also decided to update the company's marketing plan. He brought distribution in-house, created a product catalog, and started advertising his guitars in local newspapers.

The growth of the transportation industry during that time prompted Frank to brainstorm about possible ways to expand his market territory. He sensed that the most profitable opportunities for guitar sales might be in the western part of the nation rather than in the northeast. Based on that, he started traveling around the country to make sales calls in person, dramatically increasing the customer base. More shedding of the old ways.

His instincts were spot on. By the early 1900s, half of the company's revenue came from dealers on the West Coast and one music store located in Hawaii.

When Italian immigrants introduced Americans to a delightful "little guitar" called the mandolin, Martin once again recognized the signs of a changing market. His quick response and make-hay-while-the-sun-shines approach ended up being quite lucrative. The company began producing as many mandolins as possible and could barely keep up with demand.

About the same time, customers started expressing the desire for louder and more percussive instruments. Martin jumped on that idea right away and was first to meet the need. He and his team developed an industry-leading innovation: high-tensile-strength guitar strings made from steel. Then and now, artists who want that edgy, contemporary sound can't get enough of this popular invention.

But despite all the Martin family insight, they were broadsided by a trend that took a serious toll on their financial health. What did that uncertainty look like? Some of their competitors began using new machines to mass-produce guitars and offer them at significantly lower prices.

In this instance, the Martins refused to budge. Their brand was synonymous with handmade products of the finest quality. And while they knew standing firm on that point might involve losing some customers at first, they believed that serious guitar players would appreciate that difference and come back. Short-term pain, long-term gain.

They were right: The short-term wasn't pretty. Competitors started stripping away their market share, and the business was struggling. Then, in a sad double-whammy of uncertainty, the Great Depression hit.

Leaders at the company were bound and determined to keep their highly skilled and experienced workers, but they were forced to cut their pay. They resorted to discounting prices, producing guitar parts, handling more repair work, and even selling jewelry made from their raw materials.

Imagine what that looked like.

Customers were few and far between. The company's expert guitar makers were in the back room carving necklaces and pendants. Paychecks were shrinking. Morale was rock-bottom. No one would have blamed the CEO for giving up—or at least drinking a crazy amount of wine. But that's not what happened. (OK, maybe the wine part happened. Who really knows?!)

The point is, the leaders at C.F. Martin & Co. used that "unexpected downtime" to figure out how they could pivot and capture the next wave of market demand. Shed fast and keep moving! Business as usual wasn't an option.

First, they started producing an up-and-coming instrument in the 1920s called the ukulele—which was likely a "hot tip" from their music store customer in Hawaii, where it originated. By 1928, they were producing more than 5,000 ukuleles a year, which helped to keep the company afloat when other manufacturers were going under.

Also during that time, the leaders at Martin decided to focus on making some unique modifications to several of the industry's most popular guitars. They transformed a standard 12-fret guitar into a 14-fret version, giving it better range and easier access to high notes. Then they incorporated that innovation into a guitar with a larger, deeper body size, which they named the Dreadnought.

As luck would have it, the introduction of Martin's new Dreadnought coincided with the emergence of a hot, new industry: folk music (which quickly transitioned to bluegrass and country). The Dreadnought was a perfect fit, and it rapidly became Martin's best-selling model. Today it's considered an iconic instrument for musicians in every single genre.

As of 2020, C.F. Martin & Co. remains a world leader in the guitar industry, with more than 500 employees and a sprawling, 84,000-square-foot factory. The company's customer list isn't too shabby either. Its guitars are a musical mainstay for loyal musicians that span multiple decades and diverse genres, including:

- Gene Autry
- The Kingston Trio
- Elvis Presley
- Willie Nelson
- Hank Williams
- John Lennon
- Del McCoury
- David Crosby
- Paul McCartney
- Johnny Cash
- Kurt Cobain
- Eddie Vedder
- Marcus Mumford
- Neil Young
- Weezer

- Eric Clapton
- Dierks Bentley
- Colbie Caillat
- Sam Hunt
- Brad Paisley
- Elle King
- Thomas Rhett
- Lewis Capaldi
- Ed Sheeran

Even though musical tastes and instrument models have changed drastically since 1833, the Martin family responded to all of them without ever changing their dedication to exceptional quality and craftsmanship. They made fast, strategic choices that allowed them to be early to market and take full advantage of new trends. But they also knew when to "pass" if following those trends would undermine their brand.

C.F. Martin & Co. survived by keeping its finger on the pulse of the industry. Its savvy leaders turned market awareness into a tangible competitive edge that sustained them for nearly 200 years.

ANALYZING THE APPROACH

During times of uncertainty, everything changes. And it often changes at lightning speed. If we don't keep up with that, we'll quickly be left behind.

The Martin family understood that principle. They recognized the inherent value in monitoring the vast change happening outside the walls of the business: industry trends, customer preferences, and competitor strategies. They used that information to determine what was working and what wasn't. And they allowed that knowledge to guide them in their next steps. That approach led to a long history of enviable success.

Strategy #8

Shed fast and keep moving. Remain keenly aware of external influences, and don't be afraid to try something new when it makes sense.

EMBRACING FLEXIBILITY

Ten years ago, very few people could have predicted exactly what our world looks like today. The technology. The state of the global marketplace. The complex economic and regulatory environment. In fact, if you'd told me only 12 months ago that I would be presenting 98% of my keynotes and workshops through an online platform, I would have laughed. And yet, this is our current reality.

We can't plan for everything. Sometimes we end up with way more "unknowns" than "knowns." No big surprise here; that can be a terrifying time to make really big business decisions.

So which companies survive that kind of king-sized chaos? The ones with decision-makers who get really good at moving forward in the darkness of uncertainty. They don't allow themselves to become paralyzed. They look for opportunities and take them. If they make a mistake, they course-correct. And that process continues over and over and over.

Leaders within assertive organizations—just like C.F. Martin & Co.—accept that they will never have a comprehensive set of facts from which to make some strategic decisions. Even if they did, those components would probably change before the ink was dry on the proposal to the executive team. Instead, they pay close attention to what's happening. They give themselves permission to act quickly. And they forgive themselves if it doesn't work and they need to try something else.

Trial and error becomes their business as usual.

After the financial crisis in 2008, I started working with a new client in the aviation business. The leaders there didn't feel fully prepared for that bumpy ride, and they wanted to make sure that situation didn't happen again. Together we developed a strong contingency plan, designed to help the company get through whatever the next economic disaster might be. While the plan was solid and well-thought-out, the leaders have been known to update it regularly. Like...frequently. I'm talking 10–15 times in a single year.

Does that sound excessive?

Not for their industry. That marketplace is evolving at jaw-dropping speed, and they can't afford to become complacent if they want to survive the next financial dip. They have to fully embrace flexibility. And that means being committed to shed fast and keep moving.

UNDERSTANDING THE ROADBLOCKS

In a nutshell, here's the main idea: If it's not working, try something else! While that might sound like a fairly simple strategy, it's not always easy to implement.

Sometimes we have blind spots when it comes to what's not working in our companies. *("We've done that for years. It's just what we do!")* Perhaps our egos get overly involved, and it seems almost impossible to let go of our own ideas and beliefs. *("That was my initiative. I fought for it and developed it and made it happen. Why would I abandon it now?")* And other times, we're simply risk-averse. *("What if that new project ends up being a total disaster? Will we look like idiots?")*

Any way you slice it, change is uncomfortable. It's almost always easier to stick with the known rather than jumping into the unknown. Human nature at work.

But here's the problem. History is littered with examples of companies that gave in to their overly cautious tendencies. They refused to acknowledge the change happening around them, and it didn't end well. Think Polaroid. Tower Records. Circuit City. The failure to embrace reality and make some admittedly scary changes can lead to the downfall of a company, no matter how successful it has been in the past.

HIGHLIGHTING A MODERN EXAMPLE

In 2009, two friends name Jennifer Hyman and Jennifer Fleiss had an innovative business concept. What if "normal" people could get affordable access to the high-end designer clothing that famous models wear in exclusive fashion shows? That's how Rent the Runway was born—an innovative e-commerce company that, as the name suggests, rents designer clothing and accessories.

The owners immediately partnered with top designers to establish credibility and build their brand. In just four years, the company racked up 3.5 million users who "borrowed" dresses and evening gowns at a fraction of the purchase price.

Right from the start, Rent the Runway was in a constant state of evolution. The owners were perpetually analyzing the business model. What's working? What's not working? Where's the next opportunity?

That approach was a necessity, since the online clothing industry is as volatile as it is competitive. Consumer loyalties shift at lightning speed. If organizations aren't paying attention or if they get too comfortable doing the same old thing, they won't survive. Simple as that.

Rent the Runway embraced that concept. For starters, the company responded to repeated requests and expanded its offerings to include women's business attire, as well as men's and children's clothing. The online firm also experimented with retail shops in Las Vegas and New York City. When those stores were a huge hit, they opened additional stand-alone locations in Los Angeles, New York, Chicago, San Francisco and Washington, D.C.

While customer traffic was strong at the retail shops, their research indicated that nearly half of their clientele lived outside of those major cities. They began to rethink the business model and were considering a reduction of their brick-and-mortar stores.

When the global pandemic hit in the spring of 2020, the owners accelerated their plans and, by August, they announced some big changes. They would be closing all of their physical locations while beefing up their e-commerce operation. Rent the Runway was poised to offer a new, middle-tier rental option that would give subscribers more alternatives in a moderate price range.

Leaders at Rent the Runway adopted "shed fast and keep moving" as their daily mantra. They remained relevant through their willingness to change. Frequently. On a dime. And that strategy allowed them to stay a step ahead of their competitors during unprecedented seasons of uncertainty.

APPLYING THE STRATEGY

If you want your organization to become more agile, you can adopt certain processes that will help you move into the shed-fast mindset. I frequently recommend the exercise below for my clients.

EXERCISE: SEEDS, WEEDS AND NEEDS

This exercise provides a structured approach to help current and future leaders analyze their business within the existing climate. More importantly, leadership teams can use this tool to identify an unmistakable direction when everything around them seems to be in turmoil.

Let's define the components first. And yes, they're basically what you might guess. **Seeds** are the things that are working well right now (what you should expand). **Weeds** are the things that are weighing you down and preventing you from moving forward (what you should eliminate or minimize). Finally, **Needs** are your opportunities (what you should start doing to get better results).

Individually or as a leadership team, set aside 30 minutes every month or quarter to go through this exercise, and write down the answers to the following questions.

Seeds:

- What strategies and projects are currently moving the business ahead, expanding market share or increasing revenue?
- Where are you getting the most traction?
- What is producing tangible results right now?

Weeds:

- What strategies and projects feel like they are unproductive or inadequate?
- Where are you consistently hitting roadblocks?
- What could you prune back to allow for activities that are more profitable?

Needs:

- What strategies and projects could you adopt that would accelerate your success?
- What opportunities could you take advantage of?

- Are there markets and trends you could leverage now to get ahead of your competition?

Share your answers with the team, and use them as the foundation for an open group discussion. If you uncover some common answers, you may have landed on action items for immediate consideration. Filter those ideas through your core values and brand identity to determine whether these changes have enough potential to make them worth the risk. If so, go for it—with the knowledge that you can always adjust as you go.

I also encourage my clients to save their notes from these sessions and reflect on them as time passes. Those can sometimes reveal some interesting trends of their own!

When you repeat this exercise regularly, the shed-fast attitude will begin seeping into the consciousness of your leaders and team members. You can quickly and objectively assess the health of the business, even in the middle of outrageous change. And, over time, you'll get more comfortable with doing what works and eliminating what doesn't.

SEEING THE BIG PICTURE

When uncertainty is running rampant, we often can't control what's happening outside. But we *can* control our next steps.

Every choice involves a component of risk, and no one has all the right answers. But if we choose our action plan based on valid assumptions and smart insights, we can proceed toward a promising destination with the potential for great rewards.

The ability to shed fast stems from a different mindset. We have to believe that moving forward may involve making mistakes, and that's part of the learning process. But we're still *moving forward*.

Current and future leaders who do the research and have the guts to take that leap of faith, despite the unknowns, can gain a tremendous advantage. Even when they don't have all the answers, they commit to rising up and seizing new opportunities. If they get off course, they adjust. But they refuse to sit still and become paralyzed by the chaos of adversity.

Shedding fast and moving forward worked extremely well for C.F. Martin & Company—and it can be an extraordinary differentiator for you, as well.

CHAPTER TEN

Rinse and
REPEAT

BUSH BROTHERS & COMPANY FOUNDED 1908

The story began in 1904 in the charming city of Chestnut Hill, Tennessee, where a man named A.J. Bush owned the local general store, as well as a farm. He started to notice that more and more of his customers were requesting the "modern convenience" of canned foods.

Another family in the area—the Stokely brothers—already owned a canning operation just up the river, but it wasn't always easy to keep their products in stock. That's when Bush had a great idea.

What if the two families joined forces to open another cannery right across from the general store? Bush could learn about the canning business from the Stokely brothers, and the plant's close proximity to the store could accelerate sales and profit for both families. Stokely's leaders agreed to that collaborative effort, and construction got under way.

Hate to burst your bubble, but the first thing that went into the cans at this new facility was NOT beans. It was tomatoes—technically not even a vegetable. That just seems wrong to me. Back to the story...

The cannery by the general store was so profitable by 1908 that A.J. Bush was able to buy back the Stokelys' share of the business. At that point, A.J. and his two eldest sons, Fred and Claude, officially named the private-label cannery Bush Brothers & Company.

A.J. Bush was extremely passionate about his new venture, and he loved the idea of a family-owned business. For one thing, he was able to offer his sons ongoing employment, which kept them close to home. (A nice perk for their mom, Sallie!) But A.J. also knew that this company could be his legacy, passed down to future generations who would share his dedication to integrity and quality.

When World War I began in 1914, the demand for canned goods skyrocketed, and the leaders at Bush incorporated new canning and processing technologies. The facility was operating around-the-clock to keep up, and 85% of their production was diverted to feed the soldiers.

About the time that sales were dropping at the end of the war, a particularly tough growing season led to a failed tomato crop. The Bush family was hanging on to the business by a thread. Their only option was to expand production to include fruit, so they began canning peaches and blueberries. That move toward diversification ended up helping them expand their distribution throughout the southeastern US by 1930.

While the Great Depression created another surge in demand for canned goods, the Bush family was also paying close attention to their customers' changing needs—a lesson they had learned from the past. In response, they started canning less expensive foods like sauerkraut, corn and hominy, as well as the newly popular staple of pork and beans.

By 1935, the company was producing 10 million cans of vegetables per year.

I feel the need to pause here and mention that success never changed the fundamental values of the Bush family. The college-educated A.J. Bush had always been adamant about providing jobs for local neighbors and serving the community any way he could. At one point, he was even elected to the school board. His business also earned a reputation for being a responsible corporate citizen.

Cleaning and processing raw agricultural products requires massive amounts of water, but Bush was determined not to have any unnecessary waste. The company developed a system to pipe all of the wastewater to an on-site processing facility to filter out the solid material (vegetable pulp and skins). Those materials were then converted to methane that fueled the boilers and provided steam heat for the plant. The remaining water was cleaned and piped out to irrigate the farmland.

Taking those extra steps to preserve resources wasn't easy, but A.J. Bush believed it was the right thing to do. That was his trademark.

Canned goods and other grocery items gained increased visibility with the introduction of supermarkets and television advertising. In 1946, the company started branding its products under the "Bush's Best" label.

In 1952, the company's leaders made a decision that defined the future of the organization. That was the year the Bush family added *variety beans* to their product line—essentially the canned version of dry beans. This changed everything. Since beans could be grown any time of year, the company wasn't limited to the seasonal availability of other fruits and vegetables. Production could continue year-round, and the demand for canned beans was growing. This niche felt like a great fit for the company. Little did they know...

On the other hand, the leaders at Bush came to an uncomfortable realization in 1969. Customers couldn't really tell the difference between various brands of canned vegetables, so the products essentially became interchangeable commodities. Purchasing choices were made purely based on price, and customer loyalty was nonexistent. That's when third-generation CEO Condon Bush came up with a plan for product differentiation.

His concept? He wanted to make Bush's baked beans distinctive and more delicious than the alternatives using his mother's special family recipe. Cured bacon.

Brown sugar. And a secret blend of spices. Condon firmly believed that consumers would prefer the unique flavoring of Bush's beans. More importantly, they'd get in the habit of choosing that brand off the shelf—even when it costs a few cents more.

He hit the jackpot with that idea: Baked beans became the company's flagship product. And by 1990, the company was no longer a regional vegetable canner. It was a full-fledged national brand. Bush's original baked beans were the signature offering, but the company used its status to continue dominating the market with new additions like grillin' beans, chili-sauce beans, savory beans, Latin-inspired beans, organic beans, and a reduced-sodium line.

With its tremendous success, the family leaders reorganized the company to create more opportunities for employees, and they implemented a comprehensive succession plan. By 1991, they also welcomed an outside board of directors to help guide the company forward while remaining a family-owned corporation.

This wider network of leadership determined that Bush could benefit from more creative marketing—a recommendation that prompted one of the most memorable TV commercials from that era. In 1994, audiences were introduced to then-29-year-old Jay Bush and his "talking" Golden Retriever Duke, who was positioned as a less-than-trustworthy keeper of the secret family recipe. The duo became famous for their catchphrase, *"Roll that beautiful bean footage!"*

It's hard to overstate the impact of those advertisements on building the Bush brand. They were directly responsible for more than tripling the company's market share.

Still today, that popular campaign continues with fresh twists. And in 2018, when one of the Golden Retrievers cast as Duke passed away, the news went viral on Facebook with thousands of heartfelt messages and even prompted condolences from a former president. That's 24 years after the first commercial aired. Again, 24 years!

Let that sink in.

The Bush family created loyal customers across multiple generations who were emotionally invested in a *baked bean company*. They intentionally created a tangible consumer preference for a *vegetable* in a commodity market. They built a powerful brand that made customers actually *feel like family*. The strategies they used to accomplish those feats are certainly worthy of deeper study!

Today, Bush Brothers & Company is based in Knoxville, Tennessee, with numerous plant locations in several states. It processes more than 55 million pounds of beans every year and accounts for 80% of all the canned baked beans sold in America.

ANALYZING THE APPROACH

There's a reason I saved the Bush Brothers & Company case study for the end. If you look closely at the story about this amazing business, you can identify some of the winning strategies used by the family to navigate a wide range of uncertainty over more than a century. And if you think some of them sound familiar, you'd be correct!

- A.J. Bush was passionate about the power of a family business that would be passed down through the generations with a steadfast commitment to quality.

Be relentless about your vision

- The Bush family embraced the harsh realities of World War I by working 24/7 and diverting 85% of their production to feed soldiers.

Condition yourself for change

- A.J. Bush started his canning business by joining forces with a competitor, the Stokely brothers.

Get creative with collaboration

- The Bush family remained firmly committed to its customers, its community, its country and the environment.

Be clear about your core values

- The Bush family paid close attention to changing customer needs during the Great Depression and adjusted the product line to match those.

Secure your base

- The Bush family welcomed diverse ideas and support to move the company forward, welcoming an outside board of directors and an innovative marketing team.

Build your network

- The Bush family consistently demonstrated how much it valued employees and implemented a rigorous succession plan to attract top talent and keep the company viable long-term.

Strengthen your team

- The Bush family quickly diversified to begin canning peaches and blueberries when the tomato crop failed. But later, when they saw a chance to take a leadership role in the canned bean market, they were willing to let go of other fruits and vegetables to support their flagship product.

Shed fast and keep moving

- The leaders of Bush Brothers & Company made smart business decisions, year after year, which illuminates our final strategy for thriving in uncertainty.

Strategy #9

Rinse and repeat. The key to success is consistently applying all of your principles and strategies over and over, in good times and bad.

In other words...

- The Bush family implemented a combination of proven strategies as a perpetual formula for success that kept the company vital and growing since 1908.

Rinse and repeat

Since we know uncertainty is absolutely certain, consistency is the name of the game. But it's also important to remember that success is fluid, not linear.

We can't approach great business strategies like boxes to be checked off before moving on. We will undoubtedly have to use them again multiple times, in different orders, in different settings. Sometimes we have to circle back, but there's always the potential to make a giant leap ahead.

Repetition and consistency can give companies the best possible chance to survive and succeed, no matter what happens. Rinse and repeat! Do the right thing again and again, regardless of the current economy or weather report or pandemic status. That's how the Bush family achieved enduring success.

ADDING A WORD OF CAUTION

In some ways, "rinse and repeat" might seem like a minor addition to a major list. But let me assure you that this final strategy is not one to be taken lightly. It has just as much power and impact as the other eight. And in some ways, it might be the most important of all.

Why? Because no business is foolproof. It doesn't matter how long companies have been around, how awesome their products are, or how much market share they've got today. If their decision-makers don't continue to follow the strategies responsible for their success, they may find themselves in big trouble when uncertainty arrives. (And we all know, it *will* be back!)

Even the legendary businesses I've highlighted in this book aren't guaranteed to survive. They have a choice every day to follow the proven strategies or to wander off course.

It happens.

In fact, one of the companies I initially planned to feature in this book deviated from the strategies in the past few years and was met with catastrophic results. The story follows.

A man named Henry Brooks opened a clothing company called H. & D.H. Brooks & Co. in New York City in 1918. His four sons joined the business fifteen years later, and the company officially changed its name to Brooks Brothers in 1950.

Brooks Brothers quickly became an iconic brand, known for its classic American fashion. The company's innovative designers created the first seersucker suits, polo shirts and reverse-stripe ties. Their trailblazing invention of ready-to-wear suits transformed the industry. And while they kept pace with new manufacturing technology over the years, they remained true to their tailored look and high-quality standards.

Recognized as the oldest apparel brand in continuous operation within the United States, the company dressed all but four presidents dating back to James Madison. Abraham Lincoln wore a Brooks Brothers coat to the theater on the fateful night of his assassination. Other famous customers included Fred Astaire, Cary Grant, Andy Warhol, Stephen Colbert, George Clooney, the entire cast of *Mad Men*, and—fascinating fact—Kermit the Frog.

Strange but true. Brooks Brothers was tapped to make a complete, customized wardrobe for Kermit when he starred in the movie, *The Muppets*. I guess frogs sometimes need to make a fashion statement, too.

In many ways, Brooks Brothers was a shining example of a company that was following the uncertainty-fighting formula. Its leaders had a powerful vision, a collaborative approach, a commitment to core values, an impressive network, and an outstanding team.

All of that sounds great, except...

In August 2020, Brooks Brothers filed for bankruptcy. The company was sold to a group backed by mall owner Simon Property Group and a licensing firm named Authentic Brands Group.

So what happened? You guessed it. The company's leaders failed at the process of "rinse and repeat," skipping over parts of the formula that could have saved them. Instead, the hard-hitting uncertainty of a global pandemic took the company down.

Formal, tailored clothing went to the back of the closet when home offices made sweatpants and leggings perfectly acceptable attire. Customers who would normally splurge on Brooks Brothers items for weddings, proms and graduations had empty social calendars. And the company's prominent retail locations looked like ghost towns when people avoided malls to prevent exposure to the virus.

Before the pandemic became a business wrecking ball, Brooks Brothers abandoned at least two important strategies.

FAIL Strategy #2: Condition Yourself for Change

The leaders of Brooks Brothers freely admit that they maintained a relatively old-school approach to clothing design. Those more formal looks weren't appealing to younger generations, and they didn't align with changing workplace dress codes that skewed much more casual. In addition, the company downplayed the importance of having an online presence and focused instead on expanding its geographic footprint with additional retail stores.

Those choices showed that the company was failing to adapt to consumers' changing preferences for both dressing and shopping.

FAIL Strategy #5: Secure Your Base

Brooks Brothers' most dedicated customers—the ones who wore the brand as their fashion signature— were alienated when the company stopped designing and producing the beloved classics they bought again and again. These legacy customers were also highly vocal with complaints about what they perceived as the retailer's decreasing quality despite increasing prices. When their core consumers felt compelled to shop elsewhere, Brooks Brothers was in a highly vulnerable position. Add in the uncertainty and pressures of the novel coronavirus, and they didn't have a prayer of surviving.

REVIEWING THE COMPLETE FORMULA

Throughout this book, you've seen how smart businesses used some of these tried-and-true strategies to carry them through centuries of uncertainty. These tactics have a proven track record of success that reaches across huge spans of time, diverse industries and many leadership styles. So what does that mean for you?

The Bush family had the right idea.

If you intertwine all of these strategies and use them consistently as a complete formula, you can dramatically change the value you bring to the decision-making facet of your professional role. Doesn't matter if you're the president, a solopreneur or a frontline supervisor.

Understanding and applying this formula can make you an indomitable force with the ability to:

- Survive and thrive during times of uncertainty
- Uncover hidden opportunities that create a tangible competitive advantage
- Achieve lasting success through growth and transformation

On that note, let's take a look at all of the strategies pulled together into a comprehensive, uncertainty-fighting formula.

Strategy #1

Be relentless about your vision. In times of uncertainty, don't get distracted by the chaos. Maintain a laser-sharp focus on your directional goal and know where you want to be when the crisis is over.

Strategy #2

Condition yourself for change and anticipate the next wave of uncertainty. When it hits, accept reality while proactively searching for new opportunities.

Strategy #3

Get creative with collaboration during times of extreme uncertainty, even if it means working with a competitor. The synergy you produce can give both parties a better chance at survival.

Strategy #4

Be clear about your core values and commit to upholding them consistently. Don't allow uncertainty to throw you off course.

Strategy #5

Secure your base during uncertain times. Ongoing dialogue with your current customers will provide the best return on your investment and give you the guidance you need to move forward.

Strategy #6

Build your network in a strategic way, and be deliberate about making connections. Invest in those relationships with consistent contact and proactive support.

Strategy #7

Strengthen your team to create an unbreakable barrier against the threats of uncertainty. By investing in great people, you'll create a powerful competitive advantage.

Strategy #8

Shed fast and keep moving. Remain keenly aware of external influences, and don't be afraid to try something new when it makes sense.

Strategy #9

Rinse and repeat. The key to success is consistently applying all of your principles and strategies over and over, in good times and bad.

SEEING THE BIG PICTURE

The lesson here is simple but non-negotiable: Be consistent about applying all nine strategies, all the time. Think of them as a complete formula that gives you a robust, shatterproof action plan to help you survive whatever situations uncertainty dumps in your lap.

I can't possibly overemphasize the value of consistency. The strategies remain the same. The formula remains the same. You don't get a pass because of your previous success. Brooks Brothers found that out the hard way.

Your ability to survive uncertainty depends on whether you do the right things and keep doing them. Apply the formula. Rinse and repeat, indeed!

CHAPTER ELEVEN

Take Action for
BUSINESS SUCCESS

Congratulations! At this point in the book, you've learned about the individual strategies that kept companies in business for hundreds of years, even throughout grueling seasons of uncertainty. You also saw in the last chapter how those strategies can flow together to create a comprehensive formula for long-term success.

Now, I want to describe some critical guidelines for applying this all-encompassing formula in your role as a current or future leader, owner, entrepreneur or manager.

APPLYING THE FORMULA

When you deliberately make business decisions using the complete formula as a filter, you have the opportunity to demonstrate exceptional leadership in protecting your company or your employer from the heavy rains of uncertainty. The **three steps** that follow are designed to give you big-picture guidance in bringing this formula to life within your organization.

1. Be Proactive

The most effective way to utilize this uncertainty-blasting formula? Commit to implementing it BEFORE the crisis hits.

First-time rock climbers can't just wake up one morning and decide to scale El Capitan's 3,000-foot vertical granite formation in Yosemite National Park. (Well, theoretically they could, but they wouldn't get very far.) Instead, they have to train and build up their strength. Create new habits. Improve their stamina. And practice with unrelenting discipline. Then, when the day comes to face the big challenge, they are ready and they can handle whatever comes their way.

Preparing for business uncertainty is exactly the same. The greatest strategies in the world can't save a company if at least some of them aren't in place before you need them.

Bottom line? Don't wait to get started! If you need a refresher and an incentive, take a look at the uncertainty timeline in Chapter One that spans hundreds of years. Uncertainty is cyclical. It *will* return. If you're not dealing with a crisis right now, your day is coming. That's not meant to sound like a doomsday prediction or a bad attitude at work. It's just a fact. And you can determine whether your company or your employer is ready (or not) by what you do next.

No pressure.

2. Be Consistent

That's right, I'm circling back to "rinse and repeat." It's *that* critical. But I'm referring here to consistency over time and throughout the organization.

First, past success doesn't make businesses immune to future uncertainty. Be sure your company or your employer is repeatedly applying all the strategies in the formula.

Beyond that, the formula works best when it's not just used by the CEO and leadership team. It's something that should permeate a whole organization. Everyone in the company, top down, should be on board with the principles involved.

In other words, the formula ideally becomes a foundation for a corporate culture that can thrive in every environment over time. Applying the formula isn't a one-time event. It's something that is company-wide and repetitive and ongoing.

Consistency is the key. Enough said.

3. Be Methodical

So if you've been proactive and consistent in implementing the formula, the day will arrive when uncertainty makes an unwelcome entrance. You're prepared! But you want to face it with a systematic approach.

You may remember in Chapter One when I talked about **three phases** that you, your team and your company should follow to find the path forward when adversity strikes: stabilizing, growing and transforming the business. In this section, I want to provide you with some exercises to help you move through those three phases and emerge on the other side of uncertainty with strength, prosperity and a renewed focus.

EXERCISE: STABILIZE, GROW, TRANSFORM

Phase One: Stabilize the Business

Your first goal when uncertainty strikes is to do whatever it takes to make sure your business or your employer survives. That involves embracing reality, as harsh as it might be, and getting real about your options. Gather with other decision-makers for a brainstorming session and discuss the answers to these questions.

- What is the current financial condition?
- What is the current revenue? How much is stable? What can you count on?

- What are the current expenses? What, if anything, could you eliminate?
- Do the expenses exceed the revenue?
- If expenses exceed revenue, what can you do RIGHT NOW to generate more revenue?

Phase Two: Grow the Business

Once the business is stabilized, you'll have the mental bandwidth to search for growth opportunities that are inevitably lurking in the shadows. Customers still need to purchase goods and services in the middle of a crisis. They have problems that need to be solved. Smart companies identify those problems and find a way to become the solution.

Ask your leadership team and decision-makers to look beyond the current obstacles and find potential opportunities.

- Think about the uncertainty you're experiencing and the impact it has on your ability to do business. Then make a list of what the company *can* control and another list of what it *can't*. Make sure you are focusing your time and energy on what you *can* control.
- Think about the uncertainty from your customers' perspectives. What are they thinking about right now? What's worrying them? What's keeping them up at night? What is their biggest problem right now and in the months ahead?

- Identify opportunities to solve your customers' existing or anticipated problems, given the current conditions and your uncontrollable limitations. How can you be a proactive partner who adds value in the middle of a difficult time?

Phase Three: Transform the Business

You've helped to prepare your company or employer in advance for times of uncertainty. When it hits, you stabilize the business and then pursue growth opportunities. But what happens when adversity subsides?

Decision-makers in successful companies use the challenges they've experienced and the lessons they've learned to transform their businesses. They understand that the latest episode of uncertainty isn't permanent, but the impact it has on their market, their customers and their competition may be.

Gather a leadership team together to think about the best ways to take the company to the next level and evolve in a way that positions it for even greater success. The following questions can guide your discussion.

- How has your marketplace changed? Your industry? The economy?
- What's different about your customers and competitors in the aftermath of the most recent uncertainty?

- Given that impact, what needs to change about the business?
- What are three things you can do to become even more relevant in the marketplace?
- Are there new opportunities for leadership and growth?
- What will the transformed business look like? What are the keys to its success?

TAKING ACTION

The formula for thriving in uncertainty is proven to work. But it works only if you put it into action. Seems like a good time to borrow a revered quote from the wise philosophers at Nike: JUST DO IT.

Put "uncertainty-proofing" at the top of your corporate to-do list.

Form a committee. Schedule a meeting. Create an action plan using the application sections found in each strategy chapter. Your company's survival is at stake.

In many chapters of this book, I've provided a section toward the end called "Applying the Strategy." If you follow the steps described in those sections, you'll be well on your way to implementing the collection of strategies that form the uncertainty-fighting formula.

On another note, I have a surprise for you: **It's a value-added DIGITAL GIFT.**

The exercises I've included throughout the book can be extremely helpful with your implementation process. If you'd like formatted versions of these exercises to share with your teams, you can get FREE downloads from my website.

To access these full-sized handouts (8.5" x 11"), just visit **www.ValueSpeaker.com.** Click on the **Books & Courses** tab, and jump to the **Resources** category. Then follow the links for **THRIVE Resources** to see easy download instructions.

You can copy and distribute these pages as part of your work with the executive team, selected leaders or a designated "think tank." These tools can become a pivotal part of your brainstorming sessions as you take steps to implement the strategies that comprise the formula.

The following exercise worksheets are available online at www.ValueSpeaker.com:

- The Power of Focus
- Vision Quest
- Reality Check
- SKEPTIC Tool
- Value Finder
- Staying Relevant
- Pinpointing Your Purpose
- Ownership Assessment
- Targeted Development

- Seeds, Weeds and Needs
- Stabilize, Grow, Transform

As you use these tools with your team, keep in mind that *surviving* uncertainty is only the bare-minimum, baseline goal. If you want the company to *thrive*, be consistent with implementing each of the strategies in the formula. And when you do, you'll create a competitive advantage that opens the door for phenomenal growth opportunities.

CHAPTER TWELVE

Transform Your
PERSONAL LIFE

Throughout this book, you've read about businesses that have successfully tackled the challenges of uncertainty. But tucked within those corporate case studies are stories of the people who were leading the companies and working to keep them operational. The impact of wars, economic depressions and a pandemic didn't stop when they headed home at 5:00.

So what do we know about uncertainty in our personal lives? I usually think about it as "change on steroids." It's right there, linked to every phase of life—even the happiest ones.

Entering relationships. Getting married. Having children. Changing jobs. Moving to different cities. Buying a home. Dealing with aging parents. Experiencing the loss of friends and family. Facing health challenges. Divorcing. Remarrying. Retiring. And the list goes on and on.

How are we supposed to confidently navigate life when we can't predict the impact or arrival time for any of those significant changes?

That's a fair question. So think of this chapter as an unexpected bonus.

The same nine-strategy formula that helps businesses endure dark periods of uncertainty can also give you the strength and resilience you need to handle earth-shattering change on a personal level. It's an effective approach you can use yourself, and you can also share it with your children and loved ones.

In the nine sections that follow, I'll outline the personal applications for your uncertainty-fighting formula.

STRATEGY ONE: BE RELENTLESS ABOUT YOUR VISION

At age 39, I had been working in a prominent financial firm for more than five years. I'll never forget the day I got a promotion to become a C-suite executive—a role that came with all the perks. High, six-figure salary. Corner office with an amazing view. An executive assistant. Three country club memberships. I remember thinking this was the peak of my career, while simultaneously being overwhelmed by a terrible feeling of dread.

I might have gotten the job I'd been working toward for years, but deep down I knew this wasn't the life I wanted. Not by any stretch of the imagination. I didn't want to live in that city. I didn't want to spend my life in endless meetings. I didn't want to be married to my job anymore. And honestly, I had no desire to belong to one country club, much less three.

Within the span of about 10 minutes, I had a reality check of epic proportions.

I'd spent years working toward this vision for my professional life, but I somehow neglected to factor in a vision for my personal life. How did that happen? It seemed like I should have known better. And yet, there was only one thing I knew for sure at that moment. This wasn't the future I wanted.

Passing on that promotion and eventually leaving the company were some of the hardest things I have ever done. Not because I was walking out on a great opportunity, but because I was walking out with no idea of where I was headed or what to do next.

On the upside, I did come away with a valuable epiphany. My personal and professional lives were linked together, not separate entities. I needed to be relentless about a single vision that covered *all* the aspects of my life. That "a-ha moment" gave me enormous clarity and purpose for everything that followed in my career.

So what about YOUR vision for the future? Are you relentlessly pursuing a plan that is inadvertently lopsided in favor of your income-producing activities?

To apply the first strategy in the uncertainty formula to your own life as a whole, you'll need to address two key areas.

First, work to redefine your vision with an all-encompassing scope. This exercise can guide you through that process.

1. Write down what you want for your life in these five areas. What's important to you? What really matters?

    a. Health

    b. Finances

    c. Business/career

    d. Family/friends

    e. Spiritual/religious

2. Craft a new vision statement that incorporates your answers in all of those categories. It doesn't have to be perfectly worded or even make sense to anyone but you.

3. Bring your new vision to life by thinking of five words or phrases that capture the essence of success in terms of your personal characteristics. Here's a shortcut: Imagine you are overhearing a group of your friends/family/colleagues who are having a conversation about you. What words would you hope they use to describe you? (resourceful, fun-loving, caring and kind, forward-thinking, insightful, etc.)

4. Put your new vision statement with key attributes in places where you can easily access them—on your phone, on your computer, or on a notecard.

5. Commit to reading through that statement multiple times during the day, and make that a regular habit.

Now for the **second part**, which is related to your relentless focus.

Every morning when we climb out of bed, we get to choose what kind of attitude we will adopt. Positive or negative. It's not automatic; it's our decision. But the choice we make will directly impact our ability to learn, grow and succeed.

Before you roll your eyes and think that my recommendation to "be positive" is just some motivational catchphrase, I'll give you the facts.

Researchers at Stanford found that attitude absolutely affects achievement. They actually proved that your outlook matters just as much as your IQ. That's right—a good attitude helps your brain work better and increases your focus. Go ahead and extrapolate that one out. You know where I'm heading...

If you intend to have relentless focus on your vision, you'll need to start with a positive attitude. And when you do, you'll control the direction of your personal and professional life, even when tough obstacles come your way.

STRATEGY TWO: CONDITION YOURSELF FOR CHANGE

Think about how much time we invest in professional development, business planning, budget creation, and preparation for big presentations. But when it comes to our personal lives? We're more likely to "wing it."

What's wrong with that picture? With that approach, many people could theoretically be more prepared for a business merger than the birth of a child.

I remember spending months planning my wedding, but we never talked about planning for the marriage. No one really prepares you for how incredibly challenging that can be. One reason why it's difficult? A lasting marriage spans decades and will be tested through a lifetime of uncertainty. It's a no-brainer: We should spend time planning for that, as well.

It all comes back to conditioning ourselves for change on a personal level, and we need to make that part of our daily narrative. Think about it. Talk about it. Expect it. When we normalize the idea of change instead of being shocked by it every single time, we'll be better prepared to deal with it. We'll also increase the likelihood of seeing change as an opportunity rather than an obstacle.

Remember the SKEPTIC tool from Chapter Three? There's a similar version that can be used every few months to analyze your personal life, either individually or with your friends and family. The acronym—SCEPFB—isn't quite as memorable, but the idea is the same. And if you are longing for a mnemonic device to remember it, here you go: **S**ee **C**hange **E**verywhere, **P**lan **F**or **B**reakthroughs!

SCEFB Tool

- What changes do you see happening in your life in these areas?

  - Society
  - Community
  - Economics
  - Politics
  - Family/friends
  - Business/work

- What action, if any, do you need to take right now in response to these changes?
- What will be happening in the near future that you should you be planning for now?
- What deserves your close attention in the months ahead?
- How can you position yourself to take advantage of opportunities in the current/future situations to achieve personal breakthroughs?

I've made it a point in recent years to take this broader approach with my clients. I ask them to complete the

SKEPTIC tool for business and the SCEPFB tool for their personal lives. Many of them have gained valuable insights from the process, but one of my long-term clients feels like these tools basically saved his life and his business.

Ryan was 37 when I started working with him, and his business was generating around $250,000 in annual revenue. His goal was to hit $1 billion within five years. We had a strong plan in place, and he was extremely dedicated and focused. That goal was very doable.

On the other hand, Ryan's stress level was rising. He was married with three children under the age of seven. While he was busy running the company, his wife had her hands more than full trying to manage their home life.

I suggested using the SCEPFB tool every quarter and adding his wife to the brainstorming sessions. Those conversations were pivotal in helping my client focus on what was most important in his life—his marriage and his family—at a time when he could easily have been overly preoccupied with pursuing business success. Ryan credits that tool for giving him the perspective he needed.

Instead of making business revenue generation the primary goal, we were able to put the pieces in place for a balance of professional and personal financial security: planning ahead for his children's education, providing support for his sister's family after she died in a tragic accident, and helping to care for aging parents and in-laws.

Our group conversations also gave him a new appreciation for the challenges his wife faced in managing their lives while he was running the business. She happily reported that he was much more compassionate once he had a better understanding of her daily struggles.

By conditioning yourself for change in your personal life, you'll be prepared to handle the ups and downs that come with the job of "human being." You'll learn to manage the factors within your control, while accepting and compensating for those you can't.

STRATEGY THREE: GET CREATIVE ABOUT COLLABORATION

Collaboration is a necessary part of surviving in the world. Applying this strategy to our personal lives can be summed up by the old song from the Beatles: *"I get by with a little help from my friends."*

No matter how independent and determined we are, there are some situations in life that require us to ask for help. When uncertainty hits, we are infinitely stronger if we can team up with others.

To help you implement this strategy, try the following exercise. Review the challenges and opportunities you uncovered using the SCEPFB tool. Then ask yourself some targeted questions:

- Who do you know that has been through this situation before with a positive outcome? (a cancer survivor, someone who is financially sound after filing for bankruptcy, the parent of a special needs child, etc.)

- Who do you know with the skills and knowledge to handle the life changes you're experiencing? (counselor, attorney, accountant, local nonprofit, etc.)

- Who could you ask for guidance or support? (family, friends, neighbors, church family, community organizations, etc.)

- Who would be a great resource to help you solve your current challenges and take advantage of new opportunities? (personal mentor, trusted friend, industry specialist, online instructors, etc.)

I have been sharing these personal-slant strategies with my friends and family since I discovered them a few years ago. Even when the whole formula hadn't quite come together yet, I was passionate about the impact the strategies could make.

To be honest, some people weren't quite as enthusiastic about the discovery as I was—except for a young woman I met named Madison. Whenever I talked about these strategies, Madison hung on every word. She was sincerely interested, wanted to know more, and was eager to try them out.

Let me give you a little background on Madison. She was a single mother in her mid-twenties. She was working full-time while going to college, and she had no family in the area to help her take care of her son. Her plate wasn't just full; it was overflowing.

But Madison didn't let that slow her down. One of her strongest assets was her love of learning. When I shared this strategy with her as a way to create a personal life that was uncertainty-proof, she was all in and asked for my help.

Madison committed to use the SCEPFB tool and the previous questions every month for one year to help her manage the extreme uncertainty in her life. In one of our first sessions with the tool, Madison shared some information about the current challenges she was facing.

She felt stuck at her job, and she didn't believe that her boss was in her corner. She'd been passed over for two promotions. Plus, her neighborhood was starting to see a disturbing rise in crime. Break-ins were becoming more frequent, and rumors were circulating about drug deals happening just a few miles from her apartment. She was also concerned because her son's daycare program was located right in that area, while the monthly prices were continuing to climb. Bottom line, she wanted to move to a more appealing area, but she would need additional income and a more stable work situation.

After writing out those challenges, Madison began to think about whom she could work with to find solutions to those problems. One option that came to mind was talking with the other young mothers who brought their children to the same daycare. They likely had similar concerns about safety and pricing, and she wanted to get feedback about their plans for the future.

As Madison began having individual conversations with these moms, she recognized that all of them were struggling to figure out things on their own. They were craving a "support group" to bounce around ideas and get referrals for other child-related services. Madison connected all of them and formed a collaborative group of people with a common goal.

One of the moms discovered a nearby church that offered a more affordable daycare program in a safer environment. Many of the support-group mothers made the switch at the same time, which eased the transition for the children. In addition, these moms agreed to take turns providing temporary childcare when one of them needed to work and the church program was closed.

As Madison got to know more of the parents from the church program, she made some contacts that led to several job interviews. Her drive and initiative to rally this caring group of young mothers made her a leadership standout, and she earned some strong referrals from her new friends. Within six months, Madison had landed a new job with greater upward mobility and was looking for a new apartment in a nicer neighborhood.

Getting clarity on the challenges that were hampering her personal life allowed Madison to pursue creative collaboration that changed everything. She took uncertainty and transformed it into opportunity.

STRATEGY FOUR: BE CLEAR ABOUT YOUR CORE VALUES

It's tough to make decisions during uncertain times. That statement is true whether we're at work or at home. You've probably experienced that more-questions-than-answers scenario in working with a personal financial advisor.

- What will the market do next?
- Should I save money or spend it?
- What should I invest in?
- How much risk is too much?
- How will I know if I made the right choice?
- Should I pull everything out of the market and switch gears?

As you make all kinds of decisions about your personal life, keep this in mind. It's not just about finding the right answers; it's about finding the right answers FOR YOU. Every person has different standards and goals, which are basically the equivalent of core values for a business.

When you are unambiguous about your personal values and consistently use those to make decisions, you'll end up with a life that feels authentic and gratifying.

Decision-making was a real challenge for one of my clients named Alex. When I met him, he'd been a successful mortgage broker for more than twenty years, working for several firms before starting his own company. Alex recently saw an opportunity to expand his client base by forming a partnership with an older gentleman named George who had a well-established firm.

Not long after they formalized the agreement, it became obvious that Alex's new partner viewed this arrangement as a way to kick off his retirement while continuing to draw income. George started spending a serious amount of time "out of the office," overlooking important details and losing track of urgent deadlines. When he inadvertently created a problem for a client, he expected Alex to step in and save the day.

All of this was happening in 2008, as the financial crisis shattered the housing industry. Competitors were dropping like flies, and Alex was in a state of panic.

That's when Alex sought me out as a coach. He was very candid in admitting he was questioning everything about his life. Not just how to handle the sticky business situation, but also about how his business crisis was affecting his family. He was in a constant state of exhaustion, distraction and irritation, which wasn't helpful at home or at work.

Alex also went on to share that he had never really felt satisfied in his career. He had the nagging feeling that something wasn't right.

That was a brave statement, and I could tell this had been weighing heavily on him for some time. He was feeling the pressure of making decisions that would be in the best interest of his family and his clients, and he didn't want to make a mistake. No wonder he felt hopelessly stuck. The perceived risks associated with these decisions were very high.

To help Alex find some direction, we applied the "get clear on your core values" strategy. We had in-depth discussions about what was most important to him, the rules he followed for living his life, and the long-term impact he wanted to have. His legacy, so to speak. At the end of our conversation, we had developed the following list to describe Alex's core values.

1. **Maintain a healthy work/life balance:** to put his family and himself at least on par (and hopefully in front of) his work goals.

2. **Be a resource and an advocate**: to position himself as a solid supporter of his family, friends and clients.

3. **Stay innovative and creative:** to be proactive about trying new things and willing to take on calculated risks.

4. **Be fully accountable:** to take total ownership and responsibility for what is (and is not) working in his life.

5. **Keep a positive attitude and have fun:** to approach things with a good sense of humor and maintain an optimistic outlook on life.

When Alex used these core values as a litmus test to make decisions about his career and his personal life, the answers seemed surprisingly self-evident. It was time to end his brief partnership and retool his own company, taking the risk for building the type of business he had always wanted.

When you're stuck and trying to answer the big questions in life, revisit your core values. Use them as your North Star, and you'll be on track to make the right decisions for you.

STRATEGY FIVE: SECURE YOUR BASE

Applying this strategy to our professional lives involves taking care of our core customers first. Thankfully, we don't have customers in our personal lives! But we do have a base of relationships that sustain and nurture us over time. I'm referring to the loyal, true-blue people who show up for us in so many different ways.

- The sister who keeps the kids while we go on a last-minute business trip.
- The neighbor who brings us homemade chicken soup when we have the flu.

- The former college roommate who meets us at the golf course every Saturday morning at 6:30.
- The best friend who knows all of our hopes, dreams, challenges, mistakes and regrets.

Those connections are some of the most powerful tools we have during times of personal uncertainty, and that's not something we should take lightly. Before trying to go out and form new relationships, we should take deliberate steps to foster and maintain the ones we already have. When uncertainty sneaks in, those will be our lifeline.

So how can you "secure your personal base" in a structured way?

Most people have hundreds of names in their address books, ranging from acquaintances to lifelong friends. The goal is to pinpoint the ones who are the most important, relevant and influential. These are typically the folks who have a strong track record for giving you good advice, providing an honest perspective, and suggesting creative ways to solve your problems.

For many of my clients, it helps to have a more systematic process for identifying these standout supporters. Try creating an avatar with the qualities and traits of the people you'd most want to spend time with to make your life more meaningful. Here are some ideas to get you started:

- **Positive attitude:** people who see the glass half-full and find opportunity in the obstacles.

- **Hopeful:** people who see the challenges but believe that pushing through them will lead to good things.
- **Sense of humor:** people who can laugh at themselves and at tough situations.
- **Solution-oriented:** people who face a problem head-on and find a way to work around it.
- **Calm and grounded:** people who maintain their composure, even during a crisis.
- **Introspective:** people with good self-awareness and self-discipline.
- **Humble:** people who are willing to admit mistakes and show vulnerability.
- **Smart:** people who have intelligence, wisdom and common sense.
- **Supportive:** people who care about you in a proactive, tangible way.
- **Non-judgmental:** people who are open-minded and don't infuse their own standards or opinions into conversation or advice.

With that avatar in mind, look at your collection of personal relationships and make a list of 10–20 people who potentially fit that description. Then start narrowing down the options. No one will fit perfectly, but those who make the cut should check at least 70% of the boxes. Remember: you are the average of the five people you spend most of your time with. Choose carefully!

The process is fairly straightforward after that. Invest in those key relationships. Be proactive about the connections. Stay in contact, and know what's going on in their lives. Show up for them. Offer support and help whenever you can. If you consistently do those things, these people will also be there for you when life gets derailed by uncertainty.

Years ago, this strategy played a crucial role in my life. My first husband was an alcoholic who struggled with his addiction for years. After countless stints in rehab, many hospital visits and a jail sentence, he was still making bad choices. That's when I made the decision to legally separate from him.

While I wanted to remain supportive, I also needed to protect myself both emotionally and legally. It was an excruciating choice.

Compounding the challenge, a number of people in my life disagreed with my choice. They tried to convince me that he might recover if I just stayed with him. They assured me that he wouldn't have a chance if I didn't commit to helping him.

Intellectually, I knew that I'd already been trying to save him for more than a decade. No matter what I did, this was his fight. Not mine. But emotionally, these well-intentioned friends and family members were tearing me apart. Their constant second-guessing was preventing me from doing what I knew was best for me and, in the end, for my husband.

I never would have made it through this time in my life without the secure-your-base strategy. It proved invaluable. I sought support from people I already knew and trusted. They understood the complexity of the situation. They believed in me. And they were willing to support me in whatever choice I made, even if they didn't agree with it.

In addition, I chose to distance myself from those who were judgmental or disapproving of the changes I needed to make in my life. This wasn't easy, since it included my well-meaning mother and some close friends who thought I just needed to hang in there a little longer.

Ultimately, the people I chose as my personal base gave me the encouragement and support I desperately needed to start moving in a different direction. They also gave me the strength to remain committed to my decision until those who didn't initially support me came around.

Be selective in identifying your personal base. Invest the time and energy to solidify those relationships. Be there for them during times of uncertainty, and they'll gladly return the favor.

STRATEGY SIX: BUILD YOUR NETWORK

I said it in Chapter Eight, and it's worth repeating here. At any moment in time, you are only one connection away from someone who can change your life. Networking is crucial for success, although I often think it's a dying art.

Networking skills don't come naturally, and they are rarely taught. Without them, how can we learn to approach strangers and introduce ourselves? We need guidelines to help us effectively engage in balanced, two-way conversations. And we need practice, which isn't as readily available with the proliferation of digital communications. I also think social media gives us the illusion of connecting with people, but it often falls short as a way to build and strengthen relationships.

Given all of that, it's easy to let networking slide, but the consequences can be severe.

Surrounding yourself with the right people is a make-it-or-break-it policy for surviving uncertainty on a personal level, just like it is in the business world. Your network matters. Which means you need to start by expanding the way you think about networking.

Talent, skill and money can get you only so far in life. You also want to be well-connected to those who can help you solve personal problems you can't tackle by yourself.

Instead of thinking about networking as a source of business leads or a new job, consider the personal angle. That's how we find the best contractor to remodel the kitchen. That's how we get the clout to run for an office with our neighborhood association. That's how we find a great French tutor or snag an opportunity for a killer internship.

It's all about leveraging your connections to find new resources that will make your life better.

The experience of my friend Jill illustrates this point. Her son was born with a rare disease that prevented his physical and mental development. The doctors told her he would never walk or speak, and his quality of life would be limited. He would also require 24/7 care.

Her excruciating choice? Pay an obscene amount of money for caretakers or sell her company and stay home to provide the care herself.

Jill was devastated for her son, and she recognized that the situation would negatively impact her daughter as well. Her husband's work situation had not been steady, so the thought of selling her business was overwhelming. She didn't have any idea what to do. So she reached out to her network.

The first hurdle was obvious. Jill didn't know anyone else who had been diagnosed with the same rare disease. Nothing even remotely close. But she just started talking to everyone she knew. She explained the situation and asked questions. She gathered any information they could provide and requested potential connections that might lead her to answers. She followed up on the leads diligently, every single day.

Within one year, Jill found an incredible support group of parents who were going through the same unimaginable struggle. By the second year, she found a viable path to get financial support from the government to help subsidize the care for her son. She also made valuable connections with doctors, nurses and therapists who had different opinions and approaches for treating her son's disease. Because of these connections, her son ultimately learned to talk, to walk, and even attended school.

Today, Jill runs a nonprofit dedicated to helping other families in her situation. Her son is employed, lives on his own, and has a very fulfilling life.

Networking and the power of personal connections can make a world of difference.

STRATEGY SEVEN: STRENGTHEN YOUR TEAM

Wouldn't our personal lives be so much easier if we had the business equivalent of a team assigned to help us reach our goals? Unfortunately, it doesn't work that way. Sure, we have family members and friends who love us. But they have their own lives going on and may not have the bandwidth to be in our corner every minute of every day.

Even though life doesn't come with a team of people dedicated to supporting every decision we make, we can strengthen our own personal safety net so the results are almost the same.

The first step is to build your support system. Think about the people who can sustain you during times of uncertainty. Here are some ideas to get you started:

- **Mentor:** Choose a few people who are living their lives in a way that you admire. I tend to choose mentors who are 10–15 years older than I am but are willing to provide sound advice and share what has worked for them (and what hasn't).

- **Coach/counselor:** At certain times in your life, it's helpful to invest in a coach—someone who can guide you to review your situation and develop objective solutions. This can be particularly helpful for those dealing with the death of a loved one, a divorce, or a physical trauma.

- **Accountability partner:** Team up with someone who also has objectives they want to achieve. This could be anything from getting regular exercise, learning a new language or quitting a bad habit. Share your dreams, goals and challenges. Then hold each other accountable to make progress and achieve success.

- **Selected family members and friends:** Who genuinely cares about you and takes an interest in your well-being? Whose advice do you follow? Who listens to your advice?

Once you have found the right people to support you, take the time to engage with your team and strengthen it...just like you'd do in a business setting.

First, share your personal-life vision, and make sure they understand what you're trying to accomplish. If you want your team members to provide support for your journey, they need to understand the destination.

Second, make sure the people on your team know they have a voice in deciding how you choose to accomplish your goals. Give them some ownership. You aren't obligated to follow ever single piece of advice they offer, but you do want to keep your ego in check and listen to what they have to say. Learn to ask questions, listen carefully and be present in the moment.

Finally, show your team members that they matter to you. Acknowledge them and tell them how they are making a difference in your life. Send them a quick note or a special gift when appropriate to thank them for adding value to your world.

My favorite application of this strategy involves a client named Erin. She grew up in humble surroundings. And by that, I mean really poor and living in the-middle-of-nowhere Arkansas. Most of the time, her family was homeless or living in the spare room at a relative's house.

No one in Erin's family finished high school (let alone college), and no one ever had a job that paid more than minimum wage. But Erin was different. From an early age, she had a passion for learning and a true gift when it came to math and science. Still, her chances of breaking the cycle of poverty were slim, given her situation.

Slim is all she needed. Erin's support system started with a single person.

Erin's mother noticed early on that her daughter was gifted, and she wanted to somehow help her defy the odds. She scraped together the money required to enroll

Erin in the Boys & Girls Club in their rural area. That gave Erin access to tutoring, as well as some additional learning opportunities.

At school, her mother also made a point of talking to Erin's teachers in person each year. She let them know about Erin's potential, and she pushed for their help with finding someone willing to support and coach her daughter. By the time Erin graduated from high school, she had amassed a significant team of people who supported her in reaching her goals. They helped her make connections and get referrals and find new opportunities.

The investment made by Erin's "team" paid off, when she won a full-ride scholarship to Texas A&M University. Academically, she was ready for the challenge. Unfortunately, she was sometimes socially awkward compared with her classmates. She never had the typical experiences in life that would have strengthened her emotional intelligence. Her interpersonal skills were lacking, which impacted her ability to work on group projects, make presentations and compete during interviews.

Enter Beth, her astute college counselor.

Beth recognized the disconnect between Erin's abundance of intelligence and her lack of soft skills, and she searched for a mentor who would help Erin improve in this overlooked area. The mentor developed a strong relationship with Erin and, over time, taught her how to succeed in the parts of life that don't get measured on a final exam. That was exactly what she needed.

Today, Erin is a high-level director with the Texas Department of Agriculture. She also volunteers every week as a mentor for lower-income, at-risk students in the local high school.

While Erin's story is remarkable, the most amazing part might be the team of people who stepped up to the plate independently to help improve her life. Her mother. The director at the Boys & Girls Club. Her teachers. Her mentors. Her college counselor. This unlikely team contributed at different times in diverse ways to measurably transform a person's life.

Assemble a great team, and you'll find the support you need to overcome all of life's obstacles.

STRATEGY EIGHT: SHED FAST AND KEEP MOVING

The pace of change in our world is accelerating. And during uncertain times, it's not just fast; it's lightning-speed, blink-and-you'll-miss-it fast. Keeping up with that is overwhelming, to say the least. Or, as some people might put it: You snooze, you lose.

In our personal lives, we frequently respond in one of two ways. We either move so quickly or try so many things that we fail to make progress with any of them. Or we get stuck doing the same thing repeatedly while praying for a different result.

The better option is to find an objective way to look at our lives and determine whether we are getting closer to our goals or father away from them. Am I productive or just busy? Am I focused or distracted? Am I on track or falling into the same old traps?

Sometimes we can gain tremendous insights if we ask ourselves two important questions.

1. Do my actions align with my goals?

We've all been out to dinner with that friend who talks endlessly about getting in shape while eating a decadent dessert. Or listening to a relative who complains non-stop about his job but chooses to binge-watch Netflix instead of learning a new skill. We can't keep up with the pace of change if we are saying one thing and doing another.

2. Do my goals need to adjust?

Your personal life changes all the time. Are the goals you set before getting married or having a child still realistic? Are there additional opportunities available today that are more appealing? Don't get mentally stuck on reaching outdated goals. Update and move on.

My father-in-law had a lifelong best friend who was considered family. From the moment I met my husband, he was sharing insights and anecdotes from his "Uncle John." This charming man was famous for his advice about everything from catching a fish to catching a girlfriend. And while I marveled at all of his wisdom, one of his statements really stood out for me:

> "Life goes fast. Don't be afraid to change and let go when you're no longer gaining traction."

That was Uncle John's personal-life version of "shed fast and keep moving." Interestingly enough, we can use the exact same tool that works brilliantly in the workplace and apply that to our personal lives.

Take some time once a month to work through the Seeds, Weeds and Needs exercise.

Seeds:

- What are you doing in your personal life right now that is working? What's getting traction? What positive results are you getting? What's helping you move in the right direction toward your personal goals?

Weeds:

- What things are you doing in your personal life right now that are holding you back or weighing you down? What actions or attitudes are preventing you from moving forward and reaching your goals? How could you prune those back to live a happier life?

Needs:

- What things could you be doing to help you move closer to reaching your personal goals or achieving your desired outcomes? What do you need that you don't have? What opportunities could you take advantage of right now?

I love this exercise. If I'm relentlessly pursuing my vision, answering these questions helps me keep pace with the changing landscape of my life. The goals I set last year may not apply now. I have to be proactive about recognizing that and be bold about making adjustments.

Uncle John was exactly right. If it's not helping me gain traction, I can't be afraid to change.

STRATEGY NINE: RINSE AND REPEAT

One of the most undervalued concepts in life is consistency. When we build habits and rituals into our daily schedules, they become effortless because we repeat them so often. That creates progress. And progress gets us results.

The "rinse and repeat" strategy makes perfect sense for our personal lives, whether we are finding time to work out, cooking healthy meals or regularly flossing our teeth. We can't do these things once and forget about them. We have to revisit them and update them and make them part of our routines.

To demonstrate that, I want to share with you how I bake in the consistency for applying the nine strategies in our uncertainty-fighting formula.

1. My blended personal and professional **vision statement** is printed on several notecards. I read them first thing in the morning, again at lunch, and just before I shut down my office at night. Every day. It reminds me of the direction I want to go and the path I'm taking to get there.

2. At least quarterly, I **condition myself for change**. I pause to search for any upcoming shifts that could impact my personal life and brainstorm alternatives to handle them. I also spend time regularly talking with friends, family and peers to keep tabs on any shifts in their lives.

3. I am constantly looking for people with the potential to become **collaborative partners**, especially those with the information and skills to help me solve my unique challenges. Their support and counsel help me move through change at a faster pace.

4. Through it all, I use my **core values** to guide my decision-making process. If travel and work opportunities begin infringing on my

family time, I have no problem establishing limits. My priorities are very definitive.

5. One of my favorite things to do is **securing my personal base**. I am constantly sending friends postcards from my travels, texting them funny jokes, and keeping up with those relationships that matter to me. I'm fortunate to have many trusted friends, including those who also love hiking, golf and tennis. We schedule regular get-togethers to enjoy those different sports, and that time is precious for nurturing the relationships.

6. In terms of **building my network**, I take the time to meet new people. In my neighborhood, at local events, even at the grocery store. I also volunteer for projects that will allow me to make new connections, which always pumps new energy and ideas into my life.

7. I've been blessed over the years to surround myself with a **strong team** of people who have been instrumental in helping me create a rich and satisfying life. This group of go-to resources includes several close friends, the members of my mastermind group, my accountability partner and, of course, my personal mentors. I'm honored that all of these people consider themselves on "Team

Meridith," and they have graciously shared wisdom and advice that have given me so many advantages in my life.

8. This team also plays a role in helping me to **shed fast and keep moving**. They encourage me to try new things, as well as to let go of habits and rituals that aren't helping me achieve my goals.

9. Last but not least, I try to do all of these things on a continuous basis. **Rinse and repeat**. That's my plan for surviving uncertainty in the broader context of my life. I've seen it work, and I know it can work for you, too.

CONCLUSION

No matter what kind of uncertainty you're facing, at work or at home, you now have a proven solution to help you turn the tables. You've got everything you need to take control and uncover opportunity in the middle of a crisis. To grow and transform despite adversity. To succeed despite the odds.

It all comes down to one time-tested formula with nine bold strategies—the key to long-term survival for some of our country's most beloved companies.

- Be relentless about your vision.
- Condition yourself for change.
- Get creative with collaboration.
- Be clear about your core values.
- Secure your base.

- Build your network.
- Strengthen your team.
- Shed fast and keep moving.
- Rinse and repeat.

Never forget that your ability to turn uncertainty into competitive advantage is NOT related to your product, your level of market share, or even good luck. It's about your willingness to consistently follow the formula.

The secret to longevity? The simple act of discipline.

Writing this book has been a powerful journey for me, and it's an honor to share my discoveries with readers like you. I hope you'll feel the urgency for applying this formula, and I'd love to hear about your experiences with the process. If you're willing to share your success story, please contact me with details.

Wishing you strength and resilience to thrive in an uncertain world!

Meridith

ABOUT THE
AUTHOR

MERIDITH ELLIOTT POWELL

Meridith is a business strategist, keynote speaker, and award-winning author with expertise in business growth, sales, and leadership strategies. She was named **One of the Top 15 Business Growth Experts to Watch** by *Currency Fair* and **One of the Top 20 Sales Experts To Follow** by LinkedIn.

A former C-suite executive, Meridith has extensive experience in the banking, health care, and finance industries. She has earned a number of prestigious accreditations, including Master Certified Strategist, Executive Coach and Certified Speaking Professional (a designation held by less than 12% of professional speakers), and Master Certified DISC Trainer and Coach (facilitating and coaching thousands in that program).

Meridith shares her business expertise with organizations through cutting-edge messages rooted in real-life examples and real-world knowledge. She is the author of eight books, including *Winning in The Trust & Value Economy* (USA Best Book Awards finalist) and *Own It: Redefining Responsibility – Stories of Power, Freedom & Purpose*. Her latest book, *The Best Sales Book Ever!*, is positioned to be the next best-seller for high-performing salespeople and their leaders. It was honored with the Gold Award for excellence by the Nonfiction Authors Association in 2020.

www.ValueSpeaker.com

ADDITIONAL
RESOURCES

Please visit ValueSpeaker.com for a comprehensive list of services and resources available.

THRIVE EXERCISE WORKSHEETS

- The Power of Focus
- Vision Quest
- Reality Check
- SKEPTIC Tool
- Value Finder
- Staying Relevant
- Pinpointing Your Purpose
- Ownership Assessment
- Targeted Development

- Seeds, Weeds and Needs
- Stabilize, Grow, Transform

LIVE/VIRTUAL PRESENTATIONS

Emerge Successful: 7 Strategies to Redesign, Rebuild, Relaunch Your Business

Change Redefined: Strategies to Turn Uncertainty into Competitive Advantage

Leadership Redefined: Ownership, Engagement, Results!

Sales Redefined: Strategies to Open More Doors, Close More Sales

The Powerful Lessons of Struggle

DEFY: Strategies to Succeed No Matter What This Economy Does

Who Comes Next: Succession Planning Made Easy

Pure Motivation: The Gift of Struggle

OTHER BOOKS BY MERIDITH

Own It: Redefining Responsibility

Who Comes Next? Leadership Succession Planning Made Easy

The Best Sales/Leadership Book Ever

52 Sales Leadership Truths

Winning in the Trust and Value Economy

42 Rules to Turn Prospects into Customers

Mastering the Art of Success

The Confidence Plan

ONLINE COURSES

Own It: Redefining Responsibility

Who Comes Next? Leadership Succession Planning Made Easy

Business Development: Strategic Planning

Sales Enablement

Soft Skills for Sales Professionals

Selling Financial Products and Services

Selling into Industries: Manufacturing

Selling into Industries: Professional Services

Selling into Industries: Telecommunications

Consulting Foundations: Building Your Sales System

CONTACT

MERIDITH ELLIOTT POWELL

www.ValueSpeaker.com

mere@valuespeaker.com

Office: (828) 243-3510

Toll-Free: (888) 526-9998

Follow Meridith:

www.soundwisdom.com